DATE DUE			
FEB 2 8 2001			
DEC 0 3 2013			

Paperback edition
Published by Graywolf Press, 1990
2402 University Avenue
Suite 203
St. Paul, Minnesota 55114

Distributed to the trade by
Consortium Book Sales & Distribution
287 East Sixth Street
St. Paul, Minnesota 55101

LCCN 90-84134
ISBN 1-55597-142-3

Cloth edition
Available from Zygote Press
6342 Mulholland Highway
Hollywood, California 90068

Also by the author:
Tycoon Boy (*Kayak Press*, 1977; *Zygote Press*, 1985)

DISCARDED

a pastoral by Richard Grossman

Poems have appeared as follows:

Alcatraz: Sickness, Confusion, Greed, Space, Honesty, Discipline, The Lie, Change, Firefly, Beaver, Shrew, Gibbon.
The Andover Review: The Wastes, Literature, Closeness, Shyness.
The Ark River Review: Gorilla, Great Hornbill.
Attention Please: Bestiary, Passion.
The Bellingham Review: Sea Snake, Groundhog.
The Berkeley Poetry Review: Swan, Moth.
Blue Unicorn: Palimpsest, Anger, Fear, Moods, Ecstasy.
boundary 2: Vanity, Deprivation, Humanity, Thought.
Carolina Quarterly: Elephant, Mole, Butterfly.
Cedar Rock: Protoplasm, The New Art, Tightrope, The Art of Love, Poetry.
Chelsea: The Pit, The Way, The Devil.
Chicago Review: Weariness, Calm, Detail.
Concerning Poetry: Attack, Limitations.
Contact/11: Egotism, Excretion, Atonement.
Dacotah Territory: Hamster, Deer, Frog, Viper, Porcupine, Octopus, Rat, Cricket, Chimney Swift.
Dark Horse: Shame, Softness, Secrecy, Wounds, The Barrier.
Eureka Review: The Future.
The Foothill Quarterly: Ant, Virus, Lion, Vulture.
The Greenfield Review: Hate, Tissue, Fate, Tenderness, Dolphin, Trilobite, Book Louse, Gnat, Cat.
Icarus: Loss, Regret.
Images: Paranoia, Waking.
kayak: Emptiness, Darkness, Cruelty, Eden, Communication, Terror, Paralysis, Cesspool, Nobility.
The Lake Street Review: Tarantula.
The Literary Review: Disease, Immortality, Relativity.
Louisville Review: Fidelity, Victory, Inability.
Lowlands Review: Trout, Zebra, Pronghorn, Locust.
Madog (Wales): Bitterness, Lifespan, Cosmology.
Moons and Lion Tales: Owl, Oyster, Buffalo, Eagle.
The North American Review: Hog.
New Letters: Ostrich.
Paris Review: Amoeba, Roach, Hope, Plants, Pleasure.
Pembroke: Mule, Barnacle.
Poetry Northwest: Torture, Clarity.
Scree: Dodo, Flamingo, Euglena, Dog, Gull.
Some: The Brain, Desire, Depression, The Quest.
Song: Coral, Nightingale, Snail.
South Dakota Review: Raven, Wolf, Anaconda, Sea Urchin.
The Southern Poetry Review: Starfish.
The Southern Review: Morality, Self-consciousness, Difference.
Telephone: Behavior, Drama, Harmony.
Thunder Mountain Review: Squid.
Vagabond: Wandering.
WIND Literary Journal: Flow, Spring, Pain, Caution.

for Max Abe & Rosa

Greetings! Greetings!
Are you at peace? Yes I am. And your wife?
And your children? And the whole world?
And the animals?

Dogon Greeting

Every man has his cage to share
with other animals. And his consummate rage to consume
him. The cage remains.
Only the identities change within.

These animals

suffer from want, pain and confusion
like all animals. The world outside their bars

whirls in an immense blur:
the only thing constant, yet low and terrible.

The animals were lost
above the clay.

Those who lived
could not sense the old bodies

hovering there. The heat
which warmed them was bubbling off,

and when it rained,
it washed them away, parts and wholes.

The shepherd said,
Gather around, my children,

so that we may embark
on a search for what is true.

Art will be our ark.
Not the art of desire,

showing her colors so we may see
the only thing we can see,

but the art of strength,
hard, magnificent and sparse.

We shall forge
a change in the mind

and come to understand
the spirit as animal.

The difference among animals
is a figment, the shepherd said.

Between lowest and highest, a micron.
The same feelings pour on us all.

The same considerations and meanings.
Pride and vanity are like painted sky.

The effort is worthless;
advantage is a token.

But we die at each other's hands,
the animals moaned. We eat each other.

Isn't that a difference?
The shepherd was convincing:

We can only eat what we are.
Love and hunger? Little difference.

In the beginning was the Word,
said the shepherd.

The animals muttered,
Then why are they used against us?

If the Word was with God,
how did it get loose?

Now that it has multiplied like locusts,
winnowing animals in the storm,

deformed language, like a savage,
wheels a million clubs;

and we are the targets, dubbed
to remain artless. The shepherd said,

Innocence is the key to self-defense.
Language, at its best, is crystalline.

One must *know* innocence.
Then language sparkles and shines.

The shepherd played the pipes.
In the far background a tree

acknowledged the music invisibly.
The animals, meanwhile,

pored over their thoughts in another world.
Each thought separately unreachable.

Over the field the sun moved,
unmoving. It was where it was.

And in the ground bones were decaying.
The shepherd reflected, This void

contains no void. These animals
are; each spirit extends forever, full,

lonely and inexplicable.
A giant moves the sun and eats bones.

We must do what we must
and then leave all to trust.

Well, tell us, the animals replied,
what must we do? Trust whom?

Out of the din arose a chicken:
Cock-a-doodle-doo!

And a worm was munching his own
special food. A snail trudged

toward infinity. A rat took a bite
through a dark cavity. A bee hummed.

The shepherd was troubled.
Thinking unleashes alternatives;

the brain is larger than the world.
Keep to the goals that form.

Trust the norm. Courage
is the ability to define and then deny.

There is nothing more terrible than loss
which cannot be measured. Lost loss.

It was the middle of night
with no moon. The stars were bright

and plentiful. The grain
of the universe shook in the heavens.

Hearts trembled.
This slow movement is the calmest thing

that's ever happened, said the shepherd.
Powerful and simple.

Vast, deep, and completely mental.
And when we sleep, these stars,

our destiny,
burn with tender care.

Sin
is unsatisfied need.

But needs
are too far within:

They have no voice
that can truly guide them,

said the shepherd.
Morality is a leper

with porcelain skin.
We respect freedom,

replied the animals,
but have no way to get there.

Freedom is whatever
emerges, said the shepherd,

by definition,
from a perfect prison.

The animals were waiting
in the cold and wind for the sun.

When it came it drained them.
Then along came a hurricane.

Watch out! Then another downpour.
Finally it was a beautiful day,

but filled with a strange disease
and cramps. The animals were frantic.

This procession must stop! they demanded.
Each discomfort has its own special tool.

The shepherd remained cool.
Without comfort, what can be uncomfortable?

The sky, day and night,
carries woe. And hard zeal.

Pain anneals bodies. But the limits
of pain are finite and sound.

We live within a range. Comfort
is the temporary absence of plainness.

Fog covered the field.
The animals

could only find themselves.
The whiteness enclosing

every sense
in its own senselessness.

What is there to perceive
in this mist? they asked.

The singular thing
about nothing

is that it has
its limits.

The shepherd replied,
The singular thing about nothing

is that nobody
can find it.

Run through the fog.
Come close.

The more they looked,
the more intricate it became:

filled with fruit
and perfumes; filled

with tensions and exquisite names.
Every moment

detailed itself out
with interest and perfect sanity.

The shepherd said,
This vanity extends into itself

where it bends around
and means.

But whatever we learn
is only the skin

beneath which blurred organs
pulse and function.

The animals met at the lip
of depression and kissed.

Each sensed
in the other's body

bliss as a contained liquid
to be swished around and left.

There was no means of entering
the gateless gate,

beyond which
an ocean roared. They

were thereupon forced
to create another body,

a new sea that cried
out in the darkness for sun.

One foot fell
in front of another.

The eyes hungered
after the object moving through snow.

It plowed toward
the prey.

Overtook it; snapped its back.
It lay

breaded in a clump.
The animal turned its head, numb. . . .

This, said the shepherd,
is my story of ignorance.

Something happened;
something didn't.

The shepherd contemplated:
These subtle parts relate

to one another in such a way
that happiness is natural.

The beauty of my children
grazing here,

the sun that warms them
reflecting in the clear water,

the clouds
forming their mysteries

with such ease and grandeur,
and the blue sky, pure.

These were made
to make happiness possible.

Yet never have I felt
this treasure as home.

My breath moves
like mud through the ground,

and my spirit encloses
my vision

like a diamond
reddened by fire.

Every animal wanted
to get out of the way.

Births were coming along
in too great numbers.

Give us a break.
Today is a rainy day!

But there was no end
to this savage irritation.

Beauty after compelling beauty
kept fumbling along.

This song is sick!
Get me a stick!

We must constantly
succumb.

The animals were captivated.
We want the soil, they said.

We want silence:
We want to sift light and elements

silently. We want peace
and good looks. We are sick,

sick of eating each other,
and we feel guilty, meek, abused.

We were hoping survival could be
a question of location and seed.

These plants are so smug,
they can afford to breathe.

The shepherd replied:
Inside plants the same struggle rages.

Each leaf sweats.
Every root crawls down, confused.

The stars were clear.
Inspired by wonder,

the moon blundered
along its fast course.

The animals never deviated.
They were born

to the torch. Underneath,
new lava constantly roared.

We are part of the heat
in this terrible void, they thought.

Black cold is our form.
The holocaust our norm.

The animals were stiffening
like stalks in a drought. The future

blew through. Rustling snout, limb, antenna.
Firm in the present, they lifted up.

We are losing all sense of sense,
they said, and we are lost.

What is this old possibility
shirking on the edge like some jejune suspense?

Some form of innocence? We are becoming
more profound and skeptical. Dry receptacles.

This future is not enough a part of us.
Fire or rain? We wait stolid in the hard ground.

One animal stood farther away
than could be reached,

inspiring hatred. Sidling
up to the shepherd, another said,

That animal stinks. I am
on the brink of making it dead.

The shepherd said, Go ahead.
There is a large wave,

and you cannot move it.
When it breaks, you'll quake.

Its momentum formed long before
anybody could dread anybody.

Once it ebbs,
we shall both be clean.

The shepherd read from the book.
The animals shook. Why can't they say

what has to be said? they said.
They gum it up with themselves.

All that style and bombast.
Meaning! We want something we can use!

Something spare, sensible and mystical.
Something absolutely intelligible.

A gem. Of value again and again.
A stone that can be worn.

It came out;
he examined it.

It wasn't him,
nor his.

A voice
without master;

meaning;
uncast word.

I am a shepherd,
he said.

The flock has made me
what I am.

He had been
a beast

of burden,
rowing across

a sea of slush.
Occasionally,

a fish would rise
up with its wood mouth.

The horizon
lay like a towel.

Work had
no conception,

simply discipline,
the shepherd

whispered to his sheep,
asleep.

I never
waited for a sail.

It used to be, the shepherd commented,
that art was the greatest mystery,

greater than what the priests
of all the animals could ever do.

Nobody understood it
except those who could properly use it.

But the animals gleaned. It could
in no way be called boring.

Nowadays, art has been made easy;
the rules have dissolved,

and our strange voice
has ceased to move from the lungs up.

The same story is retold with the same
clumsy humor and pathos.

The animals demanded, Show us what is left!
The sun still sparkles deep in the dust!

The shepherd said, Wherever truth is sought
through form, there the great balance *begins*.

The fox sniffed, then froze.
The prairie dog stayed

at the brink of his hole.
The bear would not descend

from the tree. The beaver
kept his head in the reeds.

The shepherd said, Arise!
The emotional world of teeth

has no bite left in this field.
Let feelings blossom and blast,

unconcealed. And harmless.
One attitude binds us all:

delusion, the basis
for conflict. Beneath it,

snow swirls in the glass balls
of our emptied skulls.

One animal came to the shepherd,
distraught. When I was young, he said,

I was blind, wandering among the dead,
who fed me apples. My insides responded

to the harmonium of false designs;
my heart pounded when the witches rose.

I was confounded in baseness. My hopes
were like small birds chirping in bare trees.

I did my damage, then travelled the world
searching for somebody who could please me.

Today, I am the victim of insidious change.
The demands of love derange all direction.

I plead for familiarity, for a spirit who will simply
accept me. The animals' dishonesty and commotion

I can no longer bear emotionally. They drive me
down to distraction, confuse, suspend, detract.

I am alone on a narrowing track. At the end,
blankness waits for me, desperate in absolution.

The animals looked down.
The smaller it got,

the more life they found
until, on the smallest scale,

lives were infinitely
manifold. They said,

There are only a few
elephants and whales left,

while the protozoa
go unnumbered.

Above us, lifeless,
the stars!

Said the shepherd,
Above us, in the vacuum,

the gods roam.
Fewer and fewer,

warm and caring and daring,
our highest evolved forms,

hardly recognized,
assumed to be one.

The earth shivered delicately,
dropping the animals directly

to their knees; trees fell.
The cities surrounding the fields

boomed and then caught fire.
The shepherd put aside his lyre.

Relative to where we were, he said,
we have moved six inches to here.

Consequently, much has been destroyed.
Hurtling through space at tremendous speeds

in all directions, we arrived
at stability and lived.

This slight movement knocked
it all down. Don't frown!

The largest thing
never moves.

Step by step
they searched for the grail.

Each movement forward
meant new lies to assail, new

humiliations and gambits.
The animals revealed their torment:

In attempting to succeed
we were made to compete, to piss

in each other's grails.
At the end of the trail

our lover, the Queen, waits,
her mouth filled with cake.

Outside the group where nobody
could hear, one animal said to another,

Tie me down when no one's looking,
then do with me what you please.

Beat me or love me, cause unbearable
pleasure, or cut me, or leave me.

I don't care. I have given up
and want to be bound. I can't respond

otherwise. You must do and I obey. Pain
and pleasure exquisitely beyond escape.

What we are
bears no connection

to what we've done,
the shepherd commented.

There is no source
for fame. Even

the infamous cannot keep
the blood. The damned

are candidates for heaven;
saints revel

in their own temptation.
The animals proclaimed,

No animal was ever famous.
Nor any man. Everyone

performs the same deed.
Everyone stays empty.

Something has been bothering us
for a long while, the animals smiled.

A question of mood. We were wondering
whether destiny is nothing but how

our medium feels. The sea shines,
at times, or tumultuously roars. The sky

fills with moisture or is crystal tight.
The earth is hard or passively plowed.

Moods run through nature like waves.
Is our future the raving of surroundings?

The shepherd said, Personality moves
around us. We evolved from ghosts.

And we shall all go where the ghosts are,
destinies locked in stone and flower.

It emptied out drop by drop,
corrosive and mild. Within,

a small globe held the thin
image, presence constricted.

Each time one fell, the animals
felt their boredom temporarily

dispelled. What was emptying?
A moment held the matter briefly

and then faltered. Doom!
It was doom. The present darkened

so that each new drop now meant light,
falling where the past coagulates.

The animals were more
than peeved:

We are chained to compulsion,
they said.

Everything we have to repeat
masks sex.

We have been infected
with the need to infect,

which infects us
when our needs aren't matched,

subtly undoing us.
The shepherd responded,

Sex is more than need.
It is the basis for building

and unbuilding. It destroys
the lover who can't love.

The unneeded ones
unhanded, then consumed.

Sputtering, it almost died.
A column extending

through the core of space.
Around it the animals descended

in a vortex. There is no ground,
they screamed. We can't get down!

It burns us. It opened us
and now it burns us.

We know if it only truly enflamed,
the knowledge that surpasseth understanding

would be a tidbit in a drain.
We shall only be happy

when the universe *is* love.
The shepherd said, It is what it is.

Love can never be
two-sided. The core

will never be complete.
You will never find turf for your feet.

The animals wondered
about the Last Judgment.

What will it do to us?
They professed ignorance

of all effects. Whatever we made
was made after we left,

they surmised, all commentary
ground up by change and tossed away

among the infinite trifles.
This final decree is a straw dog

screaming in the stillness
that follows every wind!

Opinion must stay in the present,
unable to reflect

on anything: what we are
hoping to remain what we were.

Farther and farther back
the animals slipped

until they reached a point
where the cave ended.

There against the wall
they huddled like snails,

unaware of each other.
Anywhere we go we shall leave

something here
that stretches and pulls

but will not move, they said.
And at the other end

of the tunnel light
falls hysterical with threats.

What we fear the most in sleep,
the animals admitted,

is the Bottom,
where the pressure is too severe.

Nightmares come in from the sides
and pierce us there

without cover.
We are totally opened to horror. But

He is merciful,
Who allows us to rise back up

into the Real
and to reemerge whole.

Everything one builds
eventually is destroyed,

said the shepherd. Hopes,
the small, assailable dreams,

excitement of inventions
and discoveries, loveliness

and glory, all die.
Once gone, it is as if they

had never been.
Absence is complete.

The animals stared.
What we eat, we eat. What's lost?

When we sleep, we rest.
What's done is really done.

Nothing is ever lost.
Just finished.

Every contact that they made
decreased them some. Forced them

one step closer to home.
We won't go in the door!

They were stubborn.
Home will never stay here!

Whenever we enter its one room,
the walls are caught in a cyclone.

Up, up we go, toward some magic land
where the witches roam, fight.

There we must make
a journey into a vast night

of monkeys and disease.
There we must grind poppies for money

while our mothers, in another world,
laugh. My animal is making poison, each says.

My child. Homeopathic wanderer.
Never come home again!

This dream never ends. It is
a major genetic production.

At any moment it could
descend on them,

always toward the same end,
disruption.

Sometimes the limbs
were sorted out, and sometimes

an emotion atrophied.
Sometimes the home and children

went, sometimes possessions.
The animals were constantly upset.

The least we can expect
is regularity, they groaned.

There is nothing to count on.
One moment the sun

warms our skins,
the next our blood.

All the animals
yearned to be shy.

For when they undressed themselves
there was nothing there.

Difficulties, however, abounded everywhere.
Like hanks of wet leather around the neck.

Paralyzed with fear,
they were less aware. But acted.

If I stay where I am, they thought,
eventually I shall disappear.

The animals wanted to stimulate their shyness.
A secret source of grand pleasure.

This was another game
they played.

Every error and indiscretion
could be reduced to the inane.

What did it matter?
One little wayward notion, a lie

or a fling with a fellow
creature. Merely featureless extravagance!

The shepherd said,
It's what you don't do that counts.

This is the error in your game.
Forbearance, perseverance, patience.

These are made
from things undone, from things unsaid.

Several animals held a conference
on tenderness. What is it? was the subject

of discussion. It is not, they said,
simply sensuousness, nor even care.

Nor lightness of touch, nor sympathy.
It is not, nor ever will be, sexual mastery.

Tenderness is the height of activity:
a breeze moving among bodies.

They all held back something.
Perhaps it was the complete vindication

of pain that made them hold back.
But they all held back something.

The animals said, There is no way
to get an animal to give everything.

This retention is our definition,
the coldness colder than anything else,

twisting us and driving us mad.
What we keep destroys us.

The shepherd replied,
We are treacherous, greedy and cruel,

slipping slowly away immersed
in our own hands.

They confessed
eternal solitude.

Each word formed
out of a pain, had weight

they themselves
could feel. Each

statement of guilt
and frustration and loss

fell like rain
on the field.

Something shall grow here
as a result,

the shepherd thought.
More loneliness. Insult.

This lack of love is a hunger
extending through events

and culminating in my system,
the animal said. I am sure that,

once upon a time, I had it.
I was loved.

But now I strike an insane pose
among circumstances

jutting their ironies toward me
so I can't escape.

Every little act smells
of cold wit.

Life is a torment,
lacking the one most tangible thing,

which is always dying away,
coincidentally.

Four score and twenty
billion years ago,

God brought forth upon this universe
the Singularity, he said.

Absolute uniformity
before it could shift toward red.

The entire spectrum of design
and desire hung like fire

at the lip of space.
All the races and creeds,

the stark fluorescence of the galaxies,
theoretical dimensions that bend around,

were groundless, lost, unbeknownst.
A ghost with livid organs

trapped in itself.
The animals replied:

It is still there.
Within each kernel and egg

it is thick
and quiet.

Escape into a new life occurs
every time the sun moves, said the shepherd.

We are individual units of the adventure,
chosen for this mission to survive

the steady patter of moments.
Out in the rain, the animals were unimpressed:

What we are now doing is momentless;
our process is linked, can't you see?

The shepherd was pleased. Only survival
survives. The survivors always die.

This rain kills them. The stress of change
is more than any sodden adventurer can bear.

Our treasure is hidden in the dry bowels of the sun.
More than once, we shall get there.

Each animal
had gone to school,

but none had ever found a rule
to compete with reality,

which loved to eat.
This rhetoric

is rather hectic:
God God God.

No devotion;
only emotion.

False love blinds
the world.

The animals had heard
that first word

and never again
saw. The void listened.

An animal had ingested
a noxious weed.

His senses opened up
and began to bubble.

It was a trip
into the unknown

whence he'd come.
This is all flow,

he mumbled,
and I am nowhere

to be found: a current
that can't be seen.

We go through life
with our hearts tied

to what we perceive,
the animals grieved,

while one motive remains
unthought and unseen:

What ought to be is
never answered;

we are the mist
on a mirror.

The shepherd disagreed:
No thought can go unthought,

no sight unseen.
Mind and eye

know what there is
between two deaths.

Truc motive is clear
and motivationless.

Kindness is a hand in the darkness,
your own hand,

guiding you patiently toward somebody else,
the shepherd said.

He remembered how he had been trapped riding
on a fear that kept pulling down

with pangs like a pulse, squeezing his vision.
Everything had been so absurd and questionable.

Finally he had lost complete control
of his body; it was like falling into a pillow.

Tendrils of kindness
wrapped around his arms and legs and secured him.

And then his hand
gently released him. . . .

But the animals, meanwhile, had lost interest
and were going about their business,

except for a few
spinning in circles in the dust.

There was something
about the mechanics

of saying sorry
that displeased the animals.

What went wrong
should just be carried

along hidden on our backs,
they said. Being in love

with oneself
is not having to say sorry.

But, the shepherd responded,
if you lick each other's wounds,

you create a bond beyond
questions of guilt or judgment.

Apologies make tolerance tolerable,
civilized behavior less improbable.

The animals were annoyed. We have
to conserve our saliva for food,

they replied. What good is mutual esteem
if it can't dissolve what we need?

Something hopeful is about to happen,
the shepherd informed. The last train

out of town toots in the background.
Everybody who remains waves.

On that train is a long cave filled
with hanging bats and asphodel. The conductor

punches tickets until the blood drips.
Our final destination is hope, he admits.

The train sways, faithfully following track.
The animals waited. Their anxiety momentarily passed.

We've heard that there is one paying passenger,
they said. Yes, somebody on board who paid.

Looking out the window, he is afraid,
not of where he is going, but of how.

And at the point of embarkation all his friends
are no longer waving from the gates of Now.

It is our posture, they complained,
that keeps us from experiencing.

Shepherd, Shepherd,
give us the word: Tell us

how can we stand on the basis,
secure, beyond the reproach of ourselves?

How can this form of stasis that keeps
us delving and grunting be breeched?

We want to straighten up and breathe
the refined air. Sense space

in all its fairness and freedom, far
beyond the power of its digestion.

The shepherd replied,
Your concept of posture is a prison.

How do flowers consistently
maintain a proper position?

What is it we all seek?
asked the animals.

It is so obscured
by our own enthusiasm

that it is contorted
beyond recognition.

Is it love, enjoyment, increase?
No, the shepherd responded.

It is stability.
Numb peace.

Bit by bit the animal's brain
succumbed to the emptiness of the abscess.

All my vision is eaten away, he said.
My mind registers in the key of death.

My breath is poisoned. It fades
with each new effort, hopeless.

What have I done to be undone?
I was always a good animal, kind.

When the pain first dribbled across my eyes,
it was as if the sun rained apart,

feeding some dark power. Disease
is taking what it wants in a slow meal.

But when it's over, said the shepherd,
no one will be full.

Disease dies with each dying animal.
You are the host for a fresh death.

One of the animals burst
forth in anguish and love.

I cannot stand this!!
I cannot stand this!!

Please let me receive!
Please let me breathe lovingly.

Love is the only true need,
and I have been turned into it,

this need that I am.
Please return my only available kiss;

plant it on my lips, soft, warm, please.
All I want is for you to lend me

loveliness. I shall return it gladly
whenever I have to rest.

Thought and action
were one step below poetry,

the shepherd believed.
Poetry: the highest *form*!

No matter how hard I try,
nothing else can really soar,

he knew. Nothing I can say
or do is entirely beautiful.

True understanding will always be
beyond reach and speech.

It comes from the impulse
to be quiet on the page.

The animals were furious. We demand
a clearing of the mind, they ranted.

We are even willing to line up
in order to complain. That is,

to order ourselves in some new way.
This universe, for example, shifts too much.

When we endeavor to focus, beyond resolution
it sits there smug and dumb.

At the last visible point, its meaning
denies the existence of seeing!

We demand to look straight through!
We demand our rights against

the invisible! The shepherd replied,
The outside is like a drunken elf looking *in*.

What does he see reflected at the bottom?
Every limitation is a form of this reflection.

Over the brink an animal was seen
running. He would never make it.

A bird dropped from a nest.
Krill were gobbled by the whale.

There could be no mistake about it:
Every animal was destined to fail.

This inner mechanism dooms us, they wailed.
Inabilities make us edible.

Why can't we perform? There is grace
in doing things well. A marvel it is

to watch a successful escape, to see
the blood pulse heavy in the victim, contained.

Besides, our weaknesses weigh terribly,
make us lonely, misgiving, depressed.

The shepherd said, It's for the best:
Only failure can lead us toward rest.

At the corners of vision, derision
in a masque-like promenade strutted past

the modular cages where lost animals wept.
Each of these images is impregnated with something new,

they said. Newness, newness assails us. Breaks us.
We are caked with foam, our claws are wormed,

our breath stinks from the dragon; exudations
and crudities dangle in the air like old meats

under which syrups run. This is too unbearable.
The shepherd said, Once upon a time, you were bad.

You thought too hard. You crossed the river
while the banks melted. Now the current runs loose.

Your worlds develop without control or focus.
In hell, the creatures are unattacked and helpless.

An animal thought about what
he was doing, then tried to do what he thought.

The muscular effort came out short.
Each kiss was self-conscious. Each stroke

missed the mark. His own
definition became marred. Then scarred.

How can I act without premeditation?
he wondered. I'll blunder.

The shepherd asked,
How can you premeditate?

Everything must start somewhere.
Why not have it start *here*?

Clouds have no thought of rain.
Nor the earth of bodies.

Before and after are never
linked by events. Whatever happens, happens.

I am enlightened! The animal leaped.
My senses leap!

The world around me
is asleep and gone.

From head to toe
each animal was indivisible

into anything but itself.
Even the worms that fragmented,

the animalcules that reproduced
by splitting, all complex beings,

lost nothing
and had nothing to gain

by being remaindered.
We are only one life, they all said.

The shepherd and animals bowed
before something that couldn't be rejected.

Adolescents flocked together,
ashamed yet expressive

of their bodies. How can we
keep them under control?

they wondered. This thunder,
echoing in our passages,

hates to grow older. It dies
subtly when it's denied

and then is reborn into new wants.
The shepherd replied, Controls are

in the very nature of desire,
whose chaste standards

lie embedded in a world
of aging flesh.

The Muse is the one
I trust the most,

said the shepherd.
My best friend.

When I have something
to say,

before I can say it,
she says it.

When I need to be able
to confide,

she is there
by my side.

When I need to admire
someone,

she steps out of the mire,
destroying illusion.

Before the bar of animality
stood Justice

in all her forms of freedom:
growing in all directions, organic,

striving to digest all litigants.
Her scales

totally resembled mouths.
The shepherd said, Bandaged and sexy,

this queen of law
is without flaw. She is

what you want her to be.
And when your meals are properly ingested,

you may feast
on her eyes.

I shall be
whoever is necessary

in order to understand
who I am,

an animal averred,
and shall sacrifice identity

for its own sake.
What I want

is simply to be clear
to my own insight,

so I shall make
my sight itself.

The food was silent and rigid.
Bathed in its own broth.

And tinged slightly with regret, as spice.
I have now become meat,

it would have said. Finally
joined the group. Converted into it.

At this level I am properly defined.
No guesswork. Less mind.

The animals who ate plants claimed
what they ate had sinned.

There were several animals who couldn't
move, like stone.

They claimed
the air was poisoned like a dead heart.

And there were some, advanced
they thought, who claimed

the stars were the last buckets
in a vast brain. The shepherd said,

Tissue never ends. It moves
between the tooth and the victim.

Every animal is part of a larger animal.
The largest animal

ever to be
is part of somebody else.

When it became unbearable,
the speed carried them into a terrible

realm where animal warmth burned.
Then all moderation simply hurt.

Passion makes all ends victims
of means, the animals claimed,

until the means become inflamed.
Then pleasure becomes a weapon.

Escape makes no sense. The burden
of concentration is too intense.

The shepherd said, Passion is
the great teacher, opening, closing us,

whose lessons leave such massive scars.
No symbol could be more dangerous.

The pain was there and wasn't going
to leave ever, the animal said.

It would not increase when he died.
Regardless of how horribly.

If he found new love,
it would be guilty, dunked

in the past. The message
would last as long as he lasted.

Grief, unspoken hell,
deepest brand of suffering,

had sculpted the contradiction
which rested in his head:

a perfectly modeled universe
where love was never rightly acknowledged.

Seeing your child's face gnawed off
or his small body torn

so that all that are emitted are low moans
or his back broken—he struggles already dead—

or his remains left unmoving
in such a silent, final way, mixed with mud.

Or starving, his eyes
becoming less like him every day

until eventually they sink back so far they fall away,
down into his head and are snuffed.

And sometimes he dies of disease.
They are so kind and gentle and so few live:

the world's babies, a tattered heap, a meaningless
remonstrance, a dull dream of grandeur.

But the animals are above accusations.
Grief is a small, private sea.

The animals moved from place to place,
and their experiences dropped on them

as if it were raining air. They declared:
We can feel like a combustible material

the sheer loneliness.
It fills our eyes with new needs.

And at the bottom of the bin where we eat
our food is galloping

like a crack slowly forming
within ice.

It came here
with no purpose.

It wanted to grow
toward no end.

When it landed on earth,
everything became silent,

having no further need
to express itself.

The animals took advantage.
We claim this land as home,

they said and proceeded
to reform it.

That original cell
shakes within us

like a clapperless bell.
You are our new voice.

An animal huddled
underneath his barrier.

When stirred, he proclaimed
at the top of his voice:

This massive structure
composed of self-denial

has mastered all my lovers
and kept them docile.

All of my fear
and lack of confidence

is embedded in this fence.
Who will assault me

and have the courage to scale it?
Who, on the other side,

will show me my dignity?
And love me with equality?

The animals interrupted
his fine speech.

We look and look, they complained.
All we can see is the sky.

The animals were weeping copiously.
The plants had stolen their mystery

and rammed it down far beyond their roots.
The sky had sucked it up and dissipated it.

The ocean was rolling it long distances.
It was no longer theirs.

They hated themselves. It was hell.
They were now no more than animals.

What they had was on the outside. Peeked at.
It had become part of what wasn't quite.

Once we were each king in a world of meaning.
Now the world is king. We are meaningless.

The shepherd said, No! You are spotless!
Guilt is always blameless. Inconsistency

is the edge of the shadow. Where can it go
when light fills every corner of the meadow?

Everything must begin,
they reasoned.

And everything must end.
Tell us, shepherd,

how this all came to happen?
Why don't we move smoothly along?

The shepherd replied,
Things begin

because they are inherently interesting.
Things end

because they came to please and,
once unneeded,

must return
to where they always belonged.

Nothing can stay needed
for long.

We can detect them, they said,
as a subtle heaviness in blood

and bone, a weariness, scorn
for our chances yet attachment

to our main chance. These parasites
know us too well and monitor our cells.

They take our food and us with it,
filling with the sleep of our bodies.

Without mood or desire, well-placed,
they wait for us to join them.

DNA rose up in a large band
like a wedding ring over the field.

All the animals were watching.
It isn't very pretty, they exclaimed.

How do you drain it?
Is there a way to make it reflect something?

The animals, each after each,
marched proudly under the throbbing dome,

piercing the veil, as they strode,
of the verb, *to be*.

The animals were swooning.
This force that binds clouds

blinds our souls and keeps them steady,
said the shepherd. Wrapping spirits

in the source of their own light,
this brightness is equivalent to love!

Unity giving, constantly giving,
feeding pure life to the living,

it is actually too much of itself
to be noticed. Too refined and explosive.

The Grand Design, moving all animals
painfully toward perfection.

The animals complained: This light
has too many qualities, is too bright.

We wish this Grand Design were more normal.
We prefer to remain clumsy animals.

Every wheel of fortune
is a wheel, said the shepherd.

The center stays the same.
It turns but stays

where it is.
The further out you go,

the more you whizz.
Center yourselves in peace.

The animals replied,
Are you some kind of a joke?

Every action
is like a new spoke

driving us out to the rim
of experience where we're trodden.

Centrifuge
is a disease, not a choice.

Every center
is a small wheel.

An animal felt the wind
plow into his skin. It dried.

His arms withered slowly.
One by one his teeth

fell into the food.
This process is destructive, he mused,

and leaves no room for reassertion.
Why should my image fall away

from the constructions I lent it?
All I want to do is reserve

something of myself for the future.
Let my *vanity* waste away!

What do I care, if I can stay the same?
I would rather be humble and stone.

They all had on
their costumes.

I am a lily, said one.
I am a megaphone.

I am a pizza pie.
I am the Fourth of July.

I am black, white,
yellow or green!

I'm a woman!
Androgyne! An old machine!

I am not, nor ever
have been, a beast.

I know every
non-animal in the show.

I can even speak
like an animal.

Whatever we express,
claimed the artists,

must be informed with glibness.
For the future awaits

more animal art,
new fresh starts based

on new premises.
With only one defense against

creeping anonymity,
modernity—

ruthless advancement
through the ranks—

we must not take our task
too seriously.

Belligerent and cruel,
certain of the animals manhandled each other.

Shaken down, you look so different,
they sneered. The shepherd interfered:

Aggression is defeat;
God is the only one who loves a bully.

You can make it if you try,
but see: all the warmth dies around your shoulders.

Boulders of regret
are tossed off. The roads of pleasure become lost.

Softness is the medium of respect.
The animals huddled: That shepherd has a long neck!

We can see ahead of us,
like a nickelodeon, the black and white film.

Power is a physical law
that in itself creates acts.

It was the new
season when

new lives met
for the very first time.

All feelings were
as fresh as the dew.

The sky filled
with songs and dark

clouds. Shrouds
of winter exploded

up into the air
then shone. Romance

hung pregnant
in most hearts,

ready to give birth
to itself only. Romance:

turning hot
in the process.

The rooster said, The sun
comes up and I crow. Those

that awake do not blame me
for the darkness that ultimately follows.

The bee said, My sting
goes into the honey and pleases.

The shark said, What I do
has a beneficial effect on what moves

above the tide lines in the air.
The shepherd also was aware of his duty:

The infliction of pain can be as dutiful
as love. Only what cannot *not* be done

is duty. There is just one logical course:
individual duty, performed without remorse.

The animals shirked, felt stunned.
They jerked on mud, reclined,

looked around as if preoccupied.
Where is a fence to hide behind?

they thought desperately. A tree!
This flaw in beauty is separating out.

The shepherd came along.
What's wrong? he whispered.

One animal volunteered:
You see our cousin over there? Come here.

Now feed him this nut. He will eat it,
but at the other end it comes out whole.

The rumor is he's made from metal
and was sent to slave for us.

His eyes look out from the depths of electricity;
his skin is porous, breathing gas.

What is thought?
the animals asked.

The shepherd responded,
Thought is what is left

when everything else leaves.
It is emptiness defined.

It is the mind, unminded.
Impression without attitude,

leading toward *conclusion*,
the universal rule:

spontaneous logic
without topic.

Our kingdom
is a definite pyramid,

the animals avowed.
Superiority has been made

the highest virtue,
tantamount to survival.

Thus it affects our brains:
Power and hunger combine.

The shepherd replied,
Superiority is a state of mind,

nothing more. Enforcing
the equilibrium of nature and diet,

a struggle far inferior
to quiet.

Everything we do, the shepherd said,
is in some sense wrong.

And in some sense right.
Guilt is a contradiction in terms

that tries to make the past
enter the present dressed in white.

The animals weren't exactly thrilled.
How can we face the truth without our guilt?

they groaned. We would be too much alone.
Having to respond fresh and unclothed.

Punishment leads to moral definition.
Without punishment, there is only freedom.

One animal knelt
over the body of his wife.

We lived together, he cried,
through weather and danger.

She sighed when I licked her;
her system shuddered whenever

I left her. What we shared
was deep, steady, grave and light.

But when she died, her look
bore the stamp of liberty

from all that we had.
There is more to life than love.

The shepherd said,
Within the head

messages move like currents
that fill us

with a false sense
of ocean,

while with no thought
the real ocean

roars
with real emotion.

The shepherd confided, The basis
of mutual understanding is anxiety.

Those who have been purely afraid
of themselves know what it is to love.

And those who haven't don't.
Everyone needs to have been there:

in that special space
where nothing has ever made sense.

Whence compassion is essence.
Fear is so great when the universe rings

like a small bowl
that the toll is only to love.

But life is a series of ever smaller,
intenser fears, the animals complained.

One day we shall feel this, but when?
When there is no more *happening*, he said.

Why was this ludicrous ball
so enthralling, setting a precedent

for the dismal? We landed
and begged for an early dismissal.

Get us off here! they pleaded.
Let us at least feel needed

somewhere else. Round,
this makes no sense. And

we can't go up or down without limits.
Nothing is parallel. This is terrible.

Half our lives, the animals complained,
we spend running forward toward

the center, always looking for more.
Then we turn around and run the other way,

afraid of the long glide toward the end.
In the middle we feel there is something,

importance and fullness surrounded by years.
The shepherd said, Birth and death

are the two traps connected by the ropes
of our lives: an act with no hope.

The moods piled up their residue,
those small uncontrollables that hung

like pollen where they couldn't be reached.
A hashish of dead nerves and frustrations,

sournesses and fears. The animals
wanted to give up and mope. They said,

There is no conviction that can define
our actions. We are hopeless, tired.

All our aspirations now turn toward rest;
our bodies yearn for closer mire.

One animal rose
from the main group.

He struck a particular pose.
Nobody noticed.

I am serene, he muttered.
Doesn't anybody want to see?

Years of discipline
went into making me what I am.

All the orbs
spread out their cool light.

The stars configure
the meaninglessness of night,

beautifully. Each day,
something new is allowed its way.

This universe of serenity
makes me serene! I am

impregnated with sound being:
grounded, silent, seeing.

The shepherd said, Sit down, Dope.
The first rule of life is

we're all in the same boat.
It's *leaking*.

Each animal had a unique style
and had developed its own turnstile

to count the moves and impede.
The shepherd said, These moves,

although circular, have interesting grooves.
Aesthetic and moral.

Death-defying and lethal.
Other forms of consciousness are amazed.

Only we must try so hard to be.
Their actions are less engraved.

Like cattle suffering from a strange disease,
the animals lingered on the field of battle.

Up to their knees in fluids and ammo,
strange carnage of assorted limbs, muck and grim

contortions of once-cherished final moments,
they wondered if the last word had been spoken.

It hadn't. The shepherd said, What we have here
is conservation, at its most conclusive, brutally fresh.

Those that want enough shall always have—death.
This is the law of timeliness. The position here

should have veered off to the left, saving lives.
Perhaps the war would have survived to be reclashed.

Tactical error or the result of terror? No matter:
Bullets have a catalytic effect on fertilizer.

Whoever invented the Real
precluded our having to reinvent it,

all the animals squealed.
Why not simply let it be?

Rarely will it get in our way,
and when it does, that's the breaks.

Life without definition!
These are the only caveats we'll maintain:

Reproduce. Line the stomach.
Never anticipate pain.

There are three ways to be attacked,
the shepherd instructed the animals.

From outside, from inside, and not at all—
what is called the false attack.

Today, it is the inside we shall examine:
disease. When the body gives

way to something lesser than it.
We cannot run away and hide. It is

the small things fighting among themselves.
The inside fails, one item at a time,

until nothing of the outside is left
but docile land, ripe and open.

Disease makes all things within us still
and spotless from being tormented.

Holding hands in a ring.
Electricity moved

through their frames.
In the center, a flame

burning rich blue.
The shepherd swooned.

All the animals grinned.
Ecstasy is a waste,

they maintained.
It comes but goes too often.

We prefer *gaiety*.
It has an easier beginning.

Takes less away.
Ends more pleasantly.

One animal had a heightened
sense and saw the world

one second too late.
Everything was gone.

Another animal had minimized
himself and saw, too early,

the universe as palimpsest.
All action is unavoidable, he said.

Potential is an infinite jumble
of possibilities

out of which will emerge something
complete and about not to be.

The animals were bothered.
Our bodies keep working

without the same feelings
that tie us down and confuse,

they pondered. There is
no desire at the core.

Corpuscle and muscle,
vein, retina and bronchus,

all coordinate their work
without flaw or remembrance.

The shepherd commented,
Galactic miracles fill the cells.

Planets and stars also
coordinate their work:

On the highest level,
nobody wonders.

High in the trees
could be heard the breath

of genius. Like a bird
with a sore throat

or ropes groaning
in some sky harbor

holding at dock a boat
barely afloat,

this small force
hummed above them.

The shepherd said,
Even a genius cannot

truly feel this wind,
it is so still.

It is power
within the air:

the voice behind
the beautiful.

This vacancy is so vital,
said an animal, that I fill it

with magic plants, surfeit
and premonitions of disease;

I fill it with false memories,
excuses and philosophies; I feed it

until it can no longer eat.
I wish it would digest itself!

But digesting, the shepherd replied,
is something vacancy can never do.

Vacancy cannot eat anything. It
is simply the absence of food.

It came out in such crass ways.
The glands hyperactivated;

and the small betrayals and confusions.
All the illusions relating to method.

The animals departed from strict
obedience in order to fight loneliness.

Our wants are so great, turning us
into ourselves where we become isolated,

they said. Isn't there someone who can
soothe the quake, quench the fire, break

the logic of interdependence? The shepherd
reviewed the range of facts and then remarked,

You should satisfy your needs though
the world cry. Never turn the cheek away

from pleasure. Let your pain
splay in the fresh air.

Grief and deliciousness should be mainstays.
Mature in the core. Loneliness will disappear.

But, said the animals, so will the world,
and its love. We shall be lonely.

We are all sorry, they said,
for whatever we've done

that has made our lives helpless.
When we were young, we *tried*

and brought down upon ourselves
a tide of our own intent,

so that our feelings were blunted.
Now our only sharpness is the fear

of judgment and the panic of revenge.
Anything is possible punishment.

The shepherd said, No one
is ever judged. Light and dark

take their proper places in the universe.
They never transform us, never impinge.

Come back, he pleaded. Please come back!
The shepherd was worried.

I know you've been betrayed.
The animal wailed, beside himself:

They took my love away on a tray.
It is completely gone. Vanished,

what was my life in the same way
as bone or home. Rejected, disgraced,

all I want is her back, looking after me,
loving me with the only things I truly need:

warmth, tenderness and healing.
The feeling of *being* a feeling, responding.

Said the shepherd, You are blessed
with courage, to desire such loveliness.

Each animal participated with a Thing.
We are holding hands with what needs us,

they claimed. Without each of our bodies
and our beings, something would drain off, change

color and die inside. Something wise:
this Thing, a bauble,

crystal to the touch and sense. Filled
with all worth and possibility. Immense.

Small things hold the design. Our fibers
entwine with the enflamed matter, then remain

after the slow length of an individual life sinks.
See here in the ground:

The stink of the loam still resounds with richness.
My pet. My fertile gem. Companion and guest.

This Thing.
It needs me.

The problem was one
of subjectivity. The last breath

had never collapsed anything;
and this judgment could be made

without any duress or tenderness,
the shepherd commented.

The animals were incensed.
You and your crooked crook, they said.

One day *I* am going to be *dead*.
I will never die, he replied.

It made us what we are. *You*
do not exist, only *I*.

The second person
has never been part of eternity.

Dusk held the animals one step away.
At the end of certain days, squalid fire,

with its petty oranges and yellows,
rose up like a parasol. It quavered

down their spine lines and came out
untrappable. All the animals moaned

and prayed for the light to go away
so that the dark would calm down.

The trees were turning red
under the pressure. The shepherd said:

An invisible sun rises in the East!
See its black beams bright with promise!

Each sunset is the deeper dawn
that brings us back to darkness.

The animals claimed
that their shame

came from instruction.
The original sin wasn't sex

but education, they averred,
and shame was the first lesson.

Yes! said the shepherd,
Shame presupposes values,

yet in all our worlds
there is nothing

to be learned from values;
nothing is that certain.

Who should be ashamed
of what must always be?

Does a leaf learn shame
in the breeze?

It was the interpenetration
of two worlds, the shepherd said.

One where pain duplicated itself
endlessly within the imagination,

becoming tangible, and the other
a series of pleasurable sensations

that never mattered. Combined,
these formed our daily routines.

The animals replied: Introspection opens
onto the same relentless vision,

a window into a world of glass,
unbreakable and meaningless.

No one taught us how
to operate, they claimed.

Knowledge has no need
to be transmitted.

We only know that it grows,
without communicating.

Where hearts beat,
visions wheel and shine;

where brains ratiocinate,
diamonds sparkle

colloidal in the mind;
each limb stretches

where it has to be;
our eyes see what must be seen.

Knowledge
is independent of us. It is

the thinking of *one thought*.
Self-justifying; complete.

Nothing was more painful, one animal said,
than giving way. It was a barrier thicker

and harder than birth. A terror. A loathing.
A deep burning covering a deeper burning.

And then somehow it happened. An ending. Surrender.
Every follicle and pore tender to the import

of intimacy. Free and replete with desiring
and indignity. This is the highest form of pleasure:

complete, uninhibited subjection to another;
wisdom in feeling, vulnerable and loving.

They were biting nipples, maneuvering
sexual organs with provocative regularity.

They were beating, grinding, overseeing
the follies of groaning bodies.

Delight rose from their frames, liquid auras.
In the distance their aurora gleamed like moon

on sand. Sensual health, the knowledge of release,
was so potent that it could make an animal

hysterical and govern its basic actions,
the movements of gorge, cloaca, limb.

The shepherd said, There is no limit
to the muscular responses occasioned by desire.

Like globes of fantastic heat afloat
on cold black streams, they rush

through endless space. The animals said,
These sensual halos are visible throughout the universe.

What we do here has tremendous bearing
on what we are. It is a contained, bright daring.

When we are born,
we understand nothing.

We are simply *made*
and see the world also

as *made*, the living
as things;

then, with age,
qualities emerge

until we die
in a surfaceless world

of depth.
The shepherd said,

This earth and all
that breathes on earth

is universal gas.
What is always remains

what was. What we see
as qualities are forms

growing out of themselves,
born from the unborn.

An animal came to the shepherd
under an oak where leaflets

stroked and stroked the air.
Each was small, intense and similar.

The shepherd said, This tree
is at the height of visibility

and power. It towers in the sky.
But the leaflets can already sense

that their trunk isn't made from stems.
They feel tiny ravages hanging inside,

beyond the course of events.
Slowly shutting out the light.

It was black, completely black.
It surrounded them all.

This will frighten us to death!
they bawled. Someone is in there!

Who is it? asked the shepherd.
They responded: We do not recognize

the identity of our fear.
It led us into the world

and then let go.
Its face is now covered

by the faces
of everyone we know.

The multifarious elements
all combine, said the shepherd,

to create a terrible oppression,
a suffocation compounded and presented

for our edification. Elation
is the untold opposition. Beyond stress.

Here loneliness, like the blazing white
of a Mediterranean island, creeps

into our eyes and blinds us,
while on the margins of hearing the sea

spreads its harmony across
the positionless floor of nature.

Work was a blessing,
and they didn't deny it. But

they were always tired.
On the brink of something empty.

This work piles up behind us, they said.
In that sense we remain in the past.

Perhaps, replied the shepherd,
yet what you've done will last.

You've made a home for weariness.
Laboring into the future, your Host

has gained from what you've lost.
His sleep bears a delightful newness.

Life floated past,
but the image it left

was of images
that wouldn't last,

whose impressions
made no real impress

but acted like a deprivation
of sense, taking away

the defining quality.
It was through this

that all tragedies were played
as each animal dwindled

into the Outside.
The shepherd expressed pity.

We must all contribute
to what we get, they said,

until what we've got
is all that's left to give.

Fire came out of the grass;
the air stirred above the ground,

darkened, then burst into embers.
The world became larger.

The sun was gone that had burned
in them and kept them small.

Clusters of animals now felt tired.
The shepherd whispered, Sleep.

Safe within this far-flung harbor,
sleep. Float on the deep.

Every second of every minute,
every hour of every day,

every week of every year,
century, aeon, ad infinitum,

animals suffered in agony.
Show us pity! they implored God.

Let us know how You care.
Show us Your rain of understanding

and Your voice, kind. Bubbles of blood
continually rise over the horizon!

Out of the crowd an animal arose
and bellowed: God is dead!

He left you all the resonance
of His disease. He left you all

the ability to bend your knees.
Don't waste language on the dead.

Hold hands. *Stand!*
The shepherd interrupted him:

God only died out of your false pride.
He is a certain type of prayer,

always without answer.
Still here.

What they conceived of as truth
had the faintest resemblance to

a method of success. Learning
about life was related to earning,

food or whatever. The animals
used their word as a loose bond.

Why don't we get ahead? they complained.
We have nothing certain to stand on.

Honesty forms up in the mind
automatically, the shepherd said,

whenever the seer wants to *see*.
Then, what he sees is honesty.

The animals lay
on their backs,

sick for want
of love to reciprocate.

Deep, deep love,
the only true benefit.

Illegitimate,
nobody

could make them better.
This heartache

shows their worth,
said the shepherd.

One day they will melt
with no fear.

In certain realms of primate,
unlike the bugs and clams,

shells were more than shells.
Protection was a virtue.

The shepherd said,
Necessity forms its own prisons.

What we must do becomes
what we become. Sophistication

is the ultimate refinement. Then,
what we are is what we must do.

A reaction based on self-image:
evolution back toward zero.

It was like a perfume
that could be smelled

in any dell, cranny or well.
A gift of itself, a fit, a swell

of unsustainable bliss,
an identification that mixed

everything into what sensed it.
Me! Me! the animals screamed.

The first finality!
The only degree:

a pocket of wind; the
deep sky.

As children grew older,
they didn't gain but lost.

It was what went away
made them age,

until it was all gone
and they folded solid

into adulthood.
Then the fun was outside,

the excitement of the game
dead in the hide.

But games went on.
The animals said,

The universe is not seriously
clothed in all this newness.

Only players get old.
Play is continuous.

Our goal is simplicity,
said the shepherd.

If we can get underneath
the weather

to climate,
underneath the hunt to diet,

underneath our variability
to character,

underneath action and reaction
to pleasure,

the truth will seem
all that could ever have been

and complexity
unnecessary.

Everybody knew that pleasure and pain
came from the same place: the brain.

And felt the same. It is like a line
that can waver in either direction,

they claimed. Moving through the same space,
waves of feeling are their own delusion,

the interior glimpse of a circuitry
abandoned to a hostile dimension

too large, incomprehensible and real.
Our only defense has to be felt.

Life is clammy, the shepherd said,
and gives off an odor of medicine.

The closer we come to what we want,
the more ordinary it becomes. The less

desirable. Eventually it sickens,
filling our heads with grey boredom.

All excitement deadens from the inside out,
and finally leather rubs against leather:

life risen to its own surface uglier and wiser.
Then what is the answer? the animals wondered.

Pain, labor, frustration and desire,
said the shepherd, all conspire

against the monotony of our lives.
It is this constant effort that erodes

the tedium and casts it afloat, an island
in the fresh, bedazzled and heavenly ocean.

The animals were trying to form
a measurement for lifespan on some norm.

Each species has its own treaty
with time, they proclaimed.

A pact to be broken by every animal
within a range.

Yet some of us live an hour,
others a century.

Where is the justice for a mosquito
or a child that dies?

There was no time to consider,
to mature, much less to analyze.

The shepherd replied, Time
is only sufficient to itself.

Clocks lie, but never the pulse,
whose small chimes make no noise.

Like a hawk flying up high
in the light, each heart allowed itself

the exquisite pleasure of creating pain:
The hawk would never be there when viewed,

a peripheral, physical event in the blueness.
The animals said, Pain is to be loved

more deeply in order for us to kill and breed.
It must dominate our thirst and sexuality.

We cannot help it that it overboils. But,
said the shepherd, you have made pain a fiction.

The supreme act of your intelligence has been
to reduce pain to this blue nothing,

to destroy others with a minimum of feeling:
shameless, painless, complete wounding.

The father of us all died
like all fathers;

the mother of us all
was originally inside

the father,
said the shepherd,

made by men
from Dad's rib.

This new goddess
took over,

and all her children
ran for cover.

When the old lady died,
the children dined.

Thank god, they sighed,
we never again need capitalize!

Now our children can
become the gods of Gods.

One animal reached out through space.
I have taken this extension for granted,

he grimaced. How I got from here to there
through an infinity of lines.

They bent within themselves.
Everything takes the place

that it itself created. Without me,
there would be no space for me.

Even the universe, perfectly receptive,
was placed inside itself.

Space is indestructible.
Yet thought, the shepherd said,

has made no place.
Whatever it tries to occupy, it destroys.

It takes space out of space and loses it.
Thought conceives space as a friable object.

Death and food
share the same consequence,

the shepherd said.
A form of obedience.

The body turns food into mind
and then leaves behind

its own food,
what it does not need.

Death is the final
elimination of itself.

The survivor has never been
as healthy.

The animals spent the summer
watching fruit develop on the trees.

They would reach their height and then fall.
When sweet and ripe, they were taut and full.

Inside we constantly grow, said the animals.
Slowly, imperceptibly, we cover our seeds.

With knowledge. And then, packed, understanding,
we drop and the knowledge vanishes.

The seed begins again. The shepherd said,
You've missed the point. All summer you've watched

from the outside, seen the tree go back
into the ground. The seed changes!

There is true grace
to going away.

An awesome, reverent display
embodied, the shepherd proclaimed.

Age is beauty.
Every stage is decay.

We are all actors
in this glad play.

The animals replied,
It hurts!

But only within
the context of the universe,

he said. Pain
is like the wind through ripe grain.

If this ear
doesn't hear,

it won't last.
The hourglass

changes shape:
The hours

change!
Dates drop

into a bottomless
cup,

the shepherd
said.

Every moment
is disciplined

by the end,
moving

forward,
always toward

the greater
good.

How to put it out?
The shepherd had his doubts.

It wasn't really a pyre,
in spite of the old metaphor.

It was more like a heightening
of existing energy, brightening

the surface of random objects,
or like an explosion in a closet

that created, unseen,
ill-fitting clothing.

The animals were panicking
in their suits of bright bondage.

Fire! Fire! they screamed.
We thought these were bandages!

Above where the stars
spread messages

of profound fullness,
their gaze wandered

until it became endless.
The shepherd whispered:

Each of these stars
has its own life on earth,

a representative birth
that it guides til death.

What we are is tended
by our very own star!

In the far reaches '
of the shimmering galaxies,

one thing,
unthinkably powerful and blinding,

twinkles in each
baby's dream.

Every animal
at some point in time

turned into an ember,
destroyed a great mind.

Its own.
The shepherd was resigned.

Join the band
of those that tend, he offered.

Madness
with her dull wings

flaps in a neutral corner.
Anything untoward

she reproves
and musters.

For many years I thought,
an animal related,

that pleasure
could never be outdated.

It was self-defining
and irrefutable.

But then when I finally *felt* it,
it was too dimensional.

Pleasure: the mechanical
answer to meaning. Belying

a world of taste
where nerves don't function.

No joke could pass
the inspection of the animals.

Somebody's feelings were always hurt.
What we laugh at is absurdly not me,

each hastened to add quickly.
Although humor is hypothetical,

the problem isn't mine.
The shepherd reminded them:

Divine laughter laughs at the divine.
It is totally bearable, light and refined.

Technically they were all the same:
responding to the same pulse, enflamed

in the same general ways.
And when they pulsed *together*,

it was the same pulse.
The shepherd said,

The art of love is the first art:
making somebody soar.

Coming together.
All beings devolve from pleasure.

Two spirits became one in heaven
without pain,

and the entire universe was created.
Now we strike out dumbly, wounded

by ignorance. Our hearts are dead
and no longer shimmer in their pools.

And when we combine, it is matter
doing and doing and doing and doing.

The animals said, Shepherd, tell
us something that we must learn.

In that case, he replied,
there is absolutely nothing to say.

We learn not what we have to, but what we do.
Yet, if we all speak, there might leak

out some form of destiny or meaning.
The universe is so confusing and so demeaning,

only a chorus of the animals
can sing its song.

This song, as a work of art.
Everybody stark among his emotions, singing.

We shall fill this field with our rough music:
gone before it comes; never here; *everlasting*.

When I was born into the world, it was
a striped egg. I didn't ask for the furniture I got.

All day long I sang like a roller,
and at night the egg disappeared. In my whole
adult life I never touched anybody.

I ate out of a box.

I wanted to build a nest ten feet off the ground
in the Harz Mountains and praise
liberty.

Sometimes I feel I am what I am because of an unseen hand.
Maybe when I die I will go to the land of humans,

where I was before I was born.

I had a dream once lasting several months
of looking through the fields for a lost friend.
Days and nights I followed
a bear that was selfless and made out of wind.

Finally I gave up and woke with my cub,
blind and hairless, who never had heard of the savage retreat
of the grizzlies
nor of the waltz of the bulldogs
with their chains and their fires in the beargardens.

This spring I shall take my baby out
to show him a world full of cruelty and wonder.
A world that operates without a friend

and with nothing but enemies
to feed it.

When the ovipositor put me under the ground
for winter,
I made my first sound
from the egg: a cry of depression
for the futility of summer
with its vibrant, evanescent dregs.

There is no reason for my song, simply cause;
this season
with its brutal laws
sets my voice: a charm in the raw
regularity of a prison,
the manufactured delight of a toy.

A fast-aging chorus, we are bent
on happiness,
singing our own requiem
to please others: like stars, a soft tent
of loneliness,
the pulse of emptiness and mortal pleasure.

I had no need to fly
but waddled about,

the only problem I had
was doubt:

doubt of the island
and what it meant,

doubt of the fence
I couldn't see

that separated me
from sky.

When they came
with their clubs,

I finally understood
the lie.

In a world so black
its magic lanterns and small lives
are like stars tracking across an inner space,

I lurk, Architeuthis,
flailing my ware.
My knives,

my two tentacular spoons,
and my beak, a precision grinder,
await the rising of the moon,

Cachelot,
illuminant and smooth. His soft
dirigible strength runs along my length as we rise;

my crampons churn in his flesh; his teeth unmesh
my arms;
my color turns from red to white;

my eyes bathe in a different starlight;
my rasping tongue slides in;
his warm blood like ambergris glides

along the surface reflecting the moonlight.
And I wonder, What am I doing?
Is this love or hate?

The sharks at our sides sing
in the void
as our bodies rotate.

I would like to go over that golden egg story again,
one more time, and tell you
what was left inside.

The consul Manlius detected it
just before the attack of the Gauls
when the sacred geese cried murder. And nowadays

every time a Toulouse tries to take to the air there
is a residual effect that is hard to explain.

(And noodling
has a massive effect on the brain as the fat
pours into experience
and levels it like frozen soap edging toward the horizon.)

Inside everyone
there is a perfect egg that breaks and pours
a slow substance. It is hardly golden.

Once that true genius of a goose had died,
all the eggs turned white
in the farmer's eyes.

Nothing more would be born
out of gold.

During the day,
it is like ballet
as I wander under the water with zero gravity.

At night,
weight comes down on me like freight,
under the moon, surrounded by innocent cries of depravity.

Green noon,
filtered through bubbles and black streaks of silt;
white moon,
covering the fragrant grasses and acacias with milk.

I am Kiboko,
the hippo,
and these are my two lives,

separated by the finest, most fragile line
that moves along my river on the surface of time.

What is that look
so defensive and so bruised
but filled with the savor of my stew,
aromatically me yet not
quite personal?

Vanity.
A strange perfume it is.
Unsettled from my plumage as it spreads,
robust and savage.
Imperious.

My fan is there
in order to procure me what I need
through individuality wafted in air. Color.
Self-display is a form of art
like any other.

I only want to change
the illusion of change, to fit
into the world where everything perfectly matches
the diurnal brightness and clad shifting
of my radius.

Trying
to fill a default
in creation requiring my participation, spectator
to Someone Else's vision of *Himself*,
competition,

so smooth
it unfurls, this feather by feather
computation. Striking in its countless detail,
a ruthless effort to be beautiful.
Degeneration.

I wrote those plantation melodies
America loves
at the first vocable point of terrestrial
ancestry,

and now I sling them through the reeds
and at night
command the forests and the moon.

I remember what it was like in that other medium,
wrapped in goo,
how I used my now invisible tail to stay
a survivor. Today

I age, waiting to be hypnotized sensually
by a snake.
Once upon a time, there was a princess who magically
turned into a frog

and lived happily ever after with her
competent lover.

These ropes of mine have a marvelous tinge
that flashed in front of me
when I was lifted away. I landed by fate here,

where I mate and suck juice. My orb stretches beyond belief,
which is why I surprise when I kill.
Most victims don't realize
that death is simply the inability to progress.

Having made a careful study of the tragedies
which occur from hour to hour in my den,
something strange happens when life runs out of options.

(After a long discussion about resignation with my husband,
look! Now he's down on the ground with the other contain

I would like to reveal a motto
that has always held me in good stead.
I whisper it to each of my friends from the edge of the scrim
before I drop in,

and it goes like this:

There is at least one time in everyone's life
when obstacles appear insurmountable.

Some day we shall meet again
in a world without webs.

In Szechuan, where the food is hot and spicy
and the western mountains are jagged and icy,

there lives an animal called a panda,
half bear and half raccoon. You couldn't land a

panda for a zoo if you tried,
because the Commies aren't on your side.

We spend our days chewing bamboo
(pandas, not Commies), and our bright eyes lose

their toylike quality when you approach.
Everybody admires our black and white coat!

A Roosevelt got off the first shot they say
and shipped the remains back to the States.

So we prefer to remain way up in the air,
far from the USA with its neurotic fairs

where in pink and blue we sit on shelves
between kittens with bows and winking elves.

It grew out of me in such a way
that I had no control over what it did,
nor where it went,
but went on resolutely eating
and paid

strict attention to the fangs of the dogs
and stayed in the fences.

I gave up more than one bleating baby for the sake
of a good meal.
I hope to hell they weren't beating
them to bits.

Far away in the unreachable mountains, I hear
the wild one moaning
for a ticket long ago lost:

someone high up and free, jumping
in the snow,
crying for a ticket long ago lost.

The beat of the oars carries across the sea.
It was Dionysus once who created all my ancestors
out of jealousy and greed. When he threw them into the water,
he howled at intelligence; and they skirred away
in search of Apollo.

Now I see the armadas moving in strength,
coming with their knives toward the coast.
Is this a dream?

Each bubble of their wake harbors a song
sung once by dolphins: All the coral, mammals, all the denizens
of the deep, bellow to the symphony

of these boats rowing across the water toward some conquest,
toward some great fish
without a name that moves on land.
We follow along, keeping the cadence with our flukes,
drunk with radar,

measuring the grief of the impending storm
in the calm center of our vast brains.

What is beauty?
A threat.

Realization?
Death.

Emancipation?
Flight.

Relaxation?
Night.

What is horror?
A beak.

Perversity?
Technique.

Diversity?
Diet.

Absurdity?
Quiet.

All day and night we work on our lodges and plunge
holes, canals, our restaurants standing in the sun.
We make the waters rise to where the action is,

then dive where the pond takes form under our eyelids,
the various cobs stored close to where we hide our kits.

When we come into the world, we change it all around.
Through enterprise, we stand our ground,
vincible by trappers and otters,
who should only attack each other.
We are descendants of a rodent weighing seven hundred pounds.

In the fall and spring we construct impermeable ducts,
but in summer we simply float and watch
the heat and light divide the hours of the long day like a prism;

and in winter we chuckle under the snow,
delighted with the victory of capitalism
over everything disordered that flowers and flows.

It was morning, and the new sun
sparkled gold
across the ripples of a gentle sea.

I contemplated:
There has to be a way to make some money.

Perhaps if I created a gull heaven
one could reach
through a sense of aerobatic freedom,

the pigs sitting in their living rooms
would read me and soar.

I know an American I could hire!

The book is bound to be a success
if it's cute and semiliterate.

I'll bet the herd doesn't want
to consider itself a herd, but a bird.

What better way to scavenge the world?

There is no hope
for me here.
My cuticle preserves

the clarity of nutrition
as the flow appears
behind my scolex,

linear reflex
to peristalsis. I know
the packed interior

of depression, to be
at the end of digestion
where poisons

create monsters. To dream
of stale harbors
swathed in intestines;

to sink down choked,
half-eating,
half-eaten.

No animal stands between me and outer space.
I soar three thousand feet up and clasp my mate.
We dive and then break near the ground.

The sound of the bracing wind is profound
and reminds us that pride is something nobody can afford.
No fall quite ends.

These clouds fan out like black orchids over the land
where nothing remains constant. Nothing.
On the lowest level, falling simply takes a different form.

Four millennia ago, we eagles carried the pharoahs
on our broad wings to paradise. Their dark tombs
were more beautiful than any paradise could ever be,
the gilded, primping fools!

But cosmetic qualities still rule, they paint our shells,
and the blue sky is gradually emptying out its beloved eagle

My mother warned me that we wouldn't last.
She said, "The moment our race has gone,
a great flock will flee along the other side of the universe:

starry, sempiternal and finally free
of the gravity on earth."

No-see-um:
here am I and now
gone.

A dot
settling through
the eye,

residuum
of a migraine.
A true

grain.
A puncture in the air.
Creation's subtle

speck
leaking into
nowhere.

Under an alder bush,
silent,
invisible,
without odor,

I wait for my eggs
to hatch,
watching
for lynx and weasel

or a screech owl.
The best response
to danger is no response.
Nor anger.

Quiet meditation,
precise quiet:
protection through discretion,
calm,

up to the moment
of consequence.
One must
sense

another's diet,
what he truly wants,
the price he will extract
in order to buy it.

My outside is an-
ten-
nae followed by leg after leg seg-
ment
in conse-
quent
repeti-
tion,
then
inside: eye, salivary
glands,
ven-
tral nerve chord, malpighi-
an
tubule, testis, sperm duct, anal
and
gen-
ital op-
en-
ings bringing up the rear
end.

Hanging from my neck, saliva
glitters in the eyes of those with whom I converse.
My skin is bone dry. Scraggly hair
dangles from my chin and elbows.

Once I played the ape game better than any ape,
but I made too many rules
and followed them like a fool.

Nobody liked me and I knew it.

At night, all the ridicule weighed on me. I asked,
"Who could possibly love an ape?"
My muscles trembled as I pulled on my umber pyjamas.

From the heights
of a bough
overlooking the sea, I see

the sun distribute patches
of plaster
over the reef

of smooth blues and greens.
All this movement
outward

coming from the inside
of my body:
sun and ocean

tangled like marbled meat
in motion,
while only this fence

called "skin"
screens vision from flesh,
the one division

of substance.
Its gates are as infinite
as breath.

Underneath the forests of Tasmania,
like a gigantic flatfooted cat,
hiding from bushmen whose mania
is to skin and eat wombats,

I utilize my giant bucks
to deracinate roots and degrassinate
grasses. Then I chuck
it all into my hole, fascinated

with my own ability to burrow.
North in the plains the hairy-noses,
my cousins, like soft-coated burros,
hide from the same general psychosis:

those who have been liberated toward their own ends
and set adrift the children of calm islands.

The world is filled
with dishonesty,
so everything I do
is measured to protect me

from travesty.
Transparent and gentle,
graceful and refined,

each step I take is controlled
against surprise.

I am a blinkie,
glowing in the summer like a truncated twinkie,

bioluminescent
part and parcel of the effervescence

of mating.
When I feel the urge for sex, I start pulsating.

Light and life must spring from the same cause,
perhaps each other. Who knows?

Perhaps there are no causes. Only effects. Or else,
reasonless urges lighting themselves.

Bred as a tool of destruction, then unleashed,
now they call me his best friend: Dog.

I stake out a territory equal to where I live
with a certain amount of human connivance
and my own brand of piss.

There is a law that told me what to do
long before "heel" and "come" were woven into my plasma.
Now, in the depths of the backyard,
I hear the call of the wild enlisting me in a pack,
to attack.

At night, when I hear my mistress and master humping,
it is all that I can muster
to keep from spraying the linoleum. There must be a way

to rid myself of this curse
of proteinized existence
which has made me lazy, pathetic, averse—

a mass of flesh wired into a tiny house,
surrounded by pickets,
insectless grass, a clothesline, sandbox, swing set,
two scrawny trees, and a large, plastic four-wheeled mouse.

What is thanks
but a form of feeding

on someone
who is innocent?

White or dark,
it is all the same,

serving to make
your feelings

more fulfilling.
Praise be to God,

Who provides
victims and stuffing!

Inconspicuous and somewhat slimy,
at the most opportune time
I climb out on the beach, the farthest outreach of sea
life, there to shine under the moon,
pulling magically.

Then in the sand I bury my grief,
two hundred eggs and a sigh of relief for a finished cause,
the applause of the sea reminding me
of the invisible black eddies quickly retreating
into the sullen mass.

Lodged in the harsh air, time
is fleeting. I must return to the ocean with its threats of death
or die. Here near LA the grunion hunters
move along the far edge like ghosts waving
their metal hands.

My last terrestrial vision, the moon
stretching her wands like the stripes of a wild animal
across the deep. This was the high tide, through our bodies,
forcing us forward toward the rim with soft, unavoidable
bands of sleep.

Tiny birthday
candles

with wings,
or bits

of ribbon suspiciously
like plumage,

we color the air
with flowers

and dawn.
Our presence suggests

nothing
lives for long.

Stick a pin in my side and watch me prance!
My stinger hangs over the comb.

No longer able to communicate the way to honey,
I hide in my hole,

while around the interior
my image is blasting out of the pupae: our queen,
having made love once, methodically reproducing.

In three days, we shall starve the drones.

My head is overwhelmed by golden stands
waving at the edge of the beelines.
The fanners at the door to the hive are feverish,
their blank eyes indicating
I must go.

It couldn't matter less.
Already there are new creatures flying
off with my flesh.

I arose
out of blackness so dark,

only blood shed light.
Doomed to eternal struggle,

my victims remained mortal.
One night they all appeared,

obsessed by death.

They looked like bats
where their eyes were.

In the forests of India,
they stick me on horses;

in Normandy,
they cut me

at the tresses,
put an apple in my mouth.

I have been gored
from one end of the land mass

to the other, but refuse
to use the pun "bored"

when describing my attitude
toward

what the humans call
their "race."

I'll stay in the underbrush
and watch the slow finish.

On top of a hill I wait, sated
and ready for another meal: the satyr
with a problem,

but always able to chew tin til it turns
into sweater material on the outside of my skin.

What's going on in the intestines? The consummation
of diet—fluids
running up and down mountains under my belly.

My best friends call me Billy.
I am a converter with vast amounts of energy.

But where I run into trouble is
in viewing an end to all my needs. My body,
creator of excrement, wool and thought,

at one point in time will leave all behind
in a ditch:
a dying goat with a blue face,

burping ideas.

I am from the other side of evolution, aberrant stock
who challenge the myth of individuality
each time each cell breathes. There is no

personage, no demon, no personality even.
I am simply a colony.
And yet we are loosely bound, a confederacy:
choanocytes, amoebocytes, porocytes;
a melting pot where every race has no creed.

We are me:

a house filled with horror and forgetting,
our visitors picked apart and shared in a latticework of endings;
a harmless, unretractable bore; a household furnishing.

If you press me through a strainer,
I'll swim back together.

I am the one and the many, without identity,
in a conceptual

squeeze.

When I awoke for the first time,
it was as close to sleep as I
have ever been, deep in earth,
smelling the roots and damp source,
growing slowly up to the burrow mouth

where fire blasts from another source,
filling the dome with life climbing toward
a new mouth, high in the air and breathing.

Now I stay busy hunting, chipping and dreaming:
scavenger of the expendable, like all things
living; simply another form of climbing, waiting

for vein and nerve to stand up like stalks, blind,
still climbing into the heat and wind.

Rushing toward the end of existence
has led me back to the point
of destroying siblings in the womb.
The entire ocean is a tomb and I a tooth.

My only compassion is for the strong
who don't bleed. I love to flail with my two pricks
and feed my stomachs. There has never been enough

available to blunt this frenzy.
The perfect manifestation of creation,
malicious,

nothing hurts me at all. I spare no feelings
from birth til death. I move through the water
like a subtle tide
and rearrange sea life

with consummate viciousness.

I am small but full of fight.
With my tail flickering above my legs, I
am almighty in my own knobby eyes:

A migrant who roams
above the biological ground of a million eggs,
I toiled to get where I am
through vast statistical dregs.

Yet I ask myself,
"What has been the point of this total madness,
of my ten molts, each with its own attendant sadness?"

It's been two in a million simply to survive,
and it's still one out of five

I'll be served, preserved, diced, spiced
or toothpicked on ice.

Whether two-toed or
three,
there is no way to get me
out

of my tree
except
if a cat jumps me and
then

it is normally the
end.
I like to go
slow:

It is a common
way
to precisely measure
pleasure;

for in sex, feeding or any
endeavor
I could eventually
imagine,

speed has a decided
tendency
to make the wrong things
happen.

Under the hot Texas sun,
in an area that looks like the moon,

we dig out cities,
a delimited hospitality

for other dogs: where we kiss and bark
and hide in the dark

from birds and snakes.
Feeding in the brittle brakes,

our orange lenses focus on each other.
Every dog is a brother.

Why should violence be more than a joke?
Yet we tremble at our listening posts

when we hear the steps of victory,
ferret, badger and coyote,

loners looking for food,
and cattle grazing in tenderized groups:

a world of mechanized squalor,
of dog eat dog and premeditated slaughter,

that works its havoc on our simple souls,
trapped in a prim and sulfurous jello.

I am the Great Hornbill,
a giant among birds,
with my curved beak from which emits

like an old auto horn
my plaintive roar.
I dash my fruit on the ground

and feast.
In the forests
below China I paste

my wife in a tree,
feed her through a slit
until she breeds.

My ruby eye
contains a black, astonished
dot,

and in the lens I see
a panoply
of radiant jungle growth,

an immense, ebullient froth
through which I hop—
boing! boing! boing!—

on my lizard feet.
I am exotic, arbitrary,
and incomplete.

Ague, dysentery, tuberculosis, typhoid and cholera
are all my pals, the lovelies of musca domestica.
What I've done has only been to feed and excrete.
How can I help it if my specks get in the meat? After all,

when the swatter falls, I'm the mashee,
and the mashor is that huge, clumsy slob who thinks I'm dirt
They've tried everything on me
from parathion to DDT. But if things get too rough,

I'll just send for my Lord, Beelzebub,
who will descend with a new and exciting fever

from his indomitable quiver, and then we'll see
who's the maggotor, and who's the maggotee!

On the damp floor
of the forest
where
the light hasn't changed

for one million years,
I range.
My thousand eyes probe
the sweet decay.

My slime glows.
True simplicity,
when hungry.
I simply eat myself.

When attacked,
I destroy myself,
break into pieces
that crawl away.

I am matter,
every bit of which
retains
my entire character.

Sometimes my rear
parts and reforms
with no brain.
It still moves.

Hanging in a notch,
my snout moving
through the blue sky

like a windbag,
my sensitive eyes
appealing to our young,

born in July,
and to the crowd
on the ground sniffing,

I suddenly realize
that consciousness
is only process,

the universe one movement,
and I
am the manifestation

of nothing,
surrounded by
a coatimundi.

With my turning wheels and wires
and the contraptions which man has made
to keep me out of tunnels—
immaculate and fuzzy me—

I have pent up tremendous amounts of energy
which over the years has turned black.
What I am (golden hamster)
is not what you see.

All my muscles are muscles of the cage.
Hard and hopeless, they wait
to fall apart in the arms of some dumb child.
Under the ground it was moist and dark.

I heard the heartbeat there of a fragile animal
like a lark
flying through the loam.
In its beak was a freedom

you cannot clutch in your hand.

They call me Lardbucket, which is a
squeal. Funnier things, however, have been spoken.
We have seven months to figure out existence,
and then the clock runs out. I haven't

got there yet, but I will. Perhaps life is
tankage (that makes sense). Or perhaps a truffle.
I met a barrow once who told me life was a sow.

My first indication of meaning was those slats
of the creep. A refuge from weight. And
when I saw a piglet crushed by its mother, I knew
what a little space can mean. In any case,
not enough has been said on the value of Jews,
who must have been taught the secret somewhere along the wa

We hogs are smart. We know the game and the rules.
Within the game is another game

which is never worth the price of processed food.

Above and below the tree extends,
feeding from every medium—
mysterious tree,
never telling where a branch might be—
so lovely, so proportioned.

It is here near the heart I make my home,
raise my children, keep warm—
mysterious tree,
never telling where a branch might be—
where my food feeds, my song.

When I fly through the air, I seem to be free,
but freedom is permanence and ease—
mysterious tree,
never telling where a branch might be.
I make love in your arms.

We are a herd. Our stripes are fairly even,
whether we were named Williams, Pound, Eliot or Stevens.
At a point long ago, some subspecies went extinct
who couldn't stand up to the dogs but could think.

Within our groups we bray our judgments in language
no one cares to understand. When attacked,
we run for it on our hands, kicking out our hooves,
hoping nobody else can get through.

Everyone respects us who visits the zoo.
And those who don't, don't.

We are the zebras, much like one another:
some taller, some squatter.

Deep in the caves, where it always happens,
I was formed in armor that glistened with mud.
It's been all that I've been able to do to remain class conscious
of my knighthood, or night hood
as we say here in the animal kingdom where I scrabble.

I have my chinks to keep me fallible,
and every year I give birth to identical rabble.

When trouble comes I try to hide,
but if that is impossible I just get snide
inside my umbrella.

There isn't a fellah in the world who wouldn't carry around
my weight if he didn't have to jog.
Not even a dog would refuse my mail.

It's a very comfortable, very exquisite, sometimes realistic
and quite specific exoskeletal jail.

Nature was extravagant,
decking me out

like a rebus,
a custom-made job

of bird, mammal, reptile,
a Tasmanian platypus,

a furry projectile
with no teeth.

A biological pleonasm
of Freudian meat.

Lost in a pool of years, it seems my life
blends in the sweet lake,
with its plashed corners, its shaved insects, its piers,
and extends through the air
rising out of a reflection, going nowhere.

Pinioned and mute, I am an ornament, a white dream
of something inexpressibly clean:
a Thames bride, Greek god or beautiful ballerina;
mankind's prismatic view of a bird
dependent on farina.

This park is a capsule where the light falls
through waves of shadow in slow diagonals.

In the midst of a boundless storm,
an uncontrollable thunder of mass, thought and energy,
this cube of peace,

where someone wild, soft, stately and outwardly serene
floats through the angle of a willow tree.

A giant
of the earth,

storming over
bacteria, molds, yeast

and protozoa
as over clover,

feeding
in worlds

of microscopic eating
more numerous

than all the grains
of sand,

I am the behemoth
of condensation.

They say you cannot turn crap into gold,
but carp is another story. So here
I am in a transparent world wavy at the ends:

A bowl, wild celery, two snails, sand
and the All-Embracing moving between fins
is all there is,

no more. Except perhaps for a few crumbs sprinkled with ants
which rain down
whenever I hear thunder on the glass.

I wade through a world of emptiness,
bred to be empty—
a glint moving across the eye,

no more valuable, nor expensive, than a slice of pie.

From my vantage under dog hair,
I can see tubercles and polyps extending into the distance
beneath trees with dandruff for leaves.

My body yaws as the trunks waver.
My jaws sink near the roots, inject saliva
and dissolve its blood in my tube. The ground gives way
wherever I move.

Up in the branches, glossy white balls full of lice hang
ready to hatch. The woods are quiet.

There are no animals here except for these pendulous eggs
that glitter, extraterrestrial,

whose mothers long ago crawled away,
driven by the Manichean duel, Formication vs. Scratch,
to the relative safety of denser follicles.

Reddish brown,
the size of a hen,
I have a sullen
hatred of the open,

so I nest deep
in caves,
where I roost
days. At night,

I swoop
through the dark
tunnels like a bat.
There is an art

to travelling
on earth,
without sensation
as a matter of course.

Who have come to terms with death
and are willing to die
are like all dragonflies,
with no hypostatic boundary on behavior.

Our mouths are psychopathic; a maw
like a pipe; with nothing to hear; like a jet fighter, cannibal
attacking anything. Swifter than anything.

Starting underwater as an egg, then a nymph with a scoop
eating other nymphs, eggs. Then molts later
we climb out of the water and escape, having carried a new l
that escapes: Mars on wings, shining

with bars of beautiful color,
fierce, efficient, hovering above prey,

we are the exterminators,
ready to resign life soon;
but before we go, we are going to make more

room for the wind.

If you happen to be lost in the jungles of New Guinea
far from the pleasures of New York City,

and the natives are acting hot and heavy
and you feel that you need a cassowary,

a rainbow delight in the form of a bird,
a flightless tank with iron nerves,

to deliver your sodden body from evil,
from the swarming rage of ignorant cannibals,

you'll find me among the endless tangles
where I'll tear you apart with my toes at right angles.

Life is a series
of denser experiences.

The older
we become

the more familiar
we become,

the closer
together,

until nothing else
has any meaning

whatsoever.

My brethren move through the air like small tentacles:
The spirit that made me mellow even under the hand
of man, my favorite character—

the bum with his high veins
and muscles unprotective from years of mechanized slaughter,
of chemicals—has now been forged by DDT

into razors that burrow underneath the peace of others.
Deer dodge into the water; reptiles turn into stone, retreat.

The marshes boil with wigglers; the sand, alive,
crawls along the beach with new breeds turned modern.
Garlands of females after blood

descend about the plump lobes and lids
of armies lined up to be the last, cruelest,

and least significant victors.

Celebrated in rhyme and rhythm, I
am the rhino ready to die for any lost cause,
save man, whose rhetoric I could never stand.

All I want to do all day is chew:
not be hunted by a white man with blisters
who thinks I'm a moose. There are just a few

of us left in pockets. We love to romp
in the swamps and drink green buckets.

I have two rhinal tusks which always precede
a ton of meat. If you happen to get skewed,
you'll know I'm around

by the abrupt change in your mood,
caused by the rapid entry of my colossal tooth.

Larvae rain down
through the solid rain
of the sea. They are chasing me.

Yet here is a mussel:
I am over it like a large droplet,
also.

Goddamn zodiac!
Fumbling in a powerful, pluvial
coagulate.

And for what?
To indicate some fate?

Or are we simply hysterical,
veridical material

wandering through space?

I can be used to dissolve warts,
cure jaundice and dropsy, and capture forts.

Up from the South to greet the USA I came,
dragging my pouch—the most ancient mammal on earth,
ready to survive the white man, the worst.

The secrets to my duration were nestled in my birth:
a breast with only thirteen rungs, an unlucky number
for the weak who rot close to the wombs

of their unfeeling, American mothers;
and survival of the fittest right out of the egg,
the fastest social climbers with the strongest legs.

When the Bomb falls, I intend to play possum,
to sizzle and burn while my fluids run and boil,
then thirty years later to rise up and eat charcoal.

In a world of blindness,
down where there is no negligence
and no kindness,
but only a system to get on,

I am up on my hind legs, praying for rebellion
and a mood that will free me
from society's compulsions. Now what I see
I can't help eating.

It is not my own force that climbs the twig
or is the twig, that shines
wet in the leaves, in my lens:

I am an intelligent suppliant
to some over-all lack of intelligence.

Aphrodite only had to haul
around her armor
and her huge breasts, but me,

I'm stuck with all these bayonets,
my weapons
rattling around like tin cans
at my feet.

Whenever I get hun-
gry for something at the end of my spit,
I simply jet
after it,

creating my own tide. I,

at best, am a wormlike pest,
but the mollusks call me
"Peddler of Death."

Above the prairies
of South America

I rob the raptors
of their prey,

screaming like an unoiled box
snapping shut,

Caracara,
sleek slut.

Or "Polyborus plancus,"
dirty yellow

in a tree,
whose silver bill

is waiting
for someone to be pleased.

A wave within a wave,
electric and suave,
carrying a sting around
like a glove,

within every dimension
lives a form of comprehension,
defining by its needs
all boundaries.

I, a ray,
schooled in the palm
of the sea, contain
its voltage and dexterity.

Festering in the ground,
my black hairs picking up the sounds
of surface stalkers,

I wait to emerge and conquer
whatever falls into a tarantella
of knowledge. My pocket is

covered with silk;
there prey decrepitate
with minds turned to milk
thinking

they are entering a new world.
My digestive juices sluice
inside their chitin;
my mind becomes their conscience;

we merge into a new being
infinitesimally larger and wiser!
A monster
who lives for twenty-five years,

a seer
squatting in a dark den,
I dream of the deterioration
through ecstasy

of those that funnel in.

My first memory
was of being shoved out to sea,
surrounded by a dense fog of brothers and sisters.
200 million of us; we were all groaning and screaming

and the mouths came down like vats, scooping.
It was every larva for itself. Most died immediately.

Only two survived: me
and somebody on the other side of the galaxy.

Now inside my mail I mull my chances. At some point,
every molecule reaches the end of the universe and drops off.
So where am I?
Above me there is a Polynesian swimming with a knife.

His eyes are dotted with little white balls.
What is he after?
Is there hope outside the shell?

I await the answer, convinced
that life is but a spray floating endlessly in the tide.
It was only that first hectic moment

that counted.

Towering over the mess that I call home,
with my poisoned teeth and massive physiognomy,
so quick, terrifying and indiscreet,
I consume whatever comes into my view—

any larva, bug or chewable beast—
digesting my own weight in groaning flesh each day.
The world trembles when it hears the cry of the shrew.
Everything I do I try to handle my own way.

My bullying takes its course under a dome
guarded by wild birds with fanged feet.
Underneath my realm the worms roam.
Everyone sinks or rises here, eventually.

God made me into His image, demanding, resourceful, hard
with only two hours between victims; or else I starve.

Many years ago, it was the stem
reptile who lacked what I provided: protection.
So when I walked away,
it was slow, but to stay. Since then,

I have watched the species propagate
but not improve, except for a few
who were ignored or decayed like dolls in the dew.

From the Permian Age, the paludal wastes,
the carboniferous forests
(and the dinosaurs we crawled across),
and then the ice-cakes,

all life sooner or later moaned for the safety of a home
such as the kind I carry along:
a form of composition based

on deformity
and a sense of being in the proper place.

Scratch a protein and you'll get
an amino acid every time. A head that sucks
cells and a tail

that carries around life in a jail.
In the old days,
people would drop and they would say
it was a mystery, a pandemic
caused by somebody who spit on a relic. Now,

it's an entirely different matter:
the movement of tiny bubbles

in an endless batter.

I am the father of the deep,
about to die.
I gave it the good fight: 18

inches of power, there was nobody who dared
to take me on.
My most ferocious enemy was the giant sponge.

Now I sense that all the other forms are going wild.
I've seen some
swimming toward the roof while sharpening their teeth
and barking out ridiculous names for blood.
Patience

is a bore.
I've been waiting well over 300 million years
just for a better beak!

If I bury myself here in sediment,
maybe this evolution toward gore
will go away.

Yellow, black and green,
suspended over the bayou in a tree,
having had nothing to eat for 392 days
but not hungry,

I wait for something huge to come around,
to drop in,
like a tapir, peccary or caiman I could squeeze.

The vitreous air impervious to breeze,
the howl of monkeys echoes
like thunder in the leaves.

Everything here is turgid, tumid, aching to be drained,
except for me, the drainer,
so dry and patient.

The sky hangs on the land
at the time of *chuvas*, and it is poised, rufous,
to descend
like a snake on its annual victim;

and I shall watch sleepily tomorrow
as it crushes sorrow
under a torrent of soft, steaming venom.

We fish
are characterized by the persistence
of the notochord
to a great degree.

There is also a reduction
of bone
in the skeleton,

and this bone
reduction was apparent as early
as the Jurassic period,
as seen in the fossil Chondresteus.

The dermal skeleton
is also much reduced but
the tail is covered with rhomboidal scales
and on the front end of the body
in some forms

are five
lines of bony plates bearing
spines
with denticle-like structures
in between.

Somewhere
between an otter and a bear,
with goggle eyes
and white flairs,

I make my home
in Manitoba
where at night
packs of wild lobos

fill the air
with cold groans
and affrighted
screams. The bones

of my victims are piled
like logs in my wake.
I rake the forest,
defile

traps and campsites.
Regardless of weather,
my fur
doesn't frost,

and the light
from my eyes
reverberates
in the land of the lost.

I am a limey with the ability to stick,
an unswerving nationalist that will never give up the ship.

I change my coat umpteen times
in the process of getting settled. Once there,
I am the jolly hermaphrodite,
twenty-four arms attached to a kettle.

Some of my kissing cousins kiss
whales, crabs and turtles with passionate lips that won't let go.
Others conjure geese in the splash zone.

But I have always preferred a fast-moving, naval
hull.
It's a great way to sieve the world.

One day we
will come back with a new set
of babies

who won't bite
the necks that deliver them.

I remember delivering one diaper
full of phlegm
to Mrs. Nixon.

Many, many memories, but not all
that bad! I had some

with literacy
written in their eyes
and some who knew

maternity
has nothing to hide.

If somebody is in the way,
he'd better look down or else.
I sleep all winter with my eyes and mouth open,
letting the silence filter through my body, waiting

for new opportunities. My skin
is something to behold from a distance,
which I have often done.

I have a thing about the Irish, all of whom
escaped my needle grasp.
Some say I have polluted the human race.
Some say I would like to turn their women

into salamis
in despite of their failing men.

Ever since I can remember it's
been raining fire. Horrendous winds

sigh within.

The small, pinlike creatures that are siphoned
into the storm cry out

for someone to love them as they dissolve.

Giustizia mosse il mio alto fattore,
purveyor of eternal agony.

Within the calm precincts of my shell,
hell remains discrete.

What is it
about the sea
that is appealing?

We are all inferior
to each other,
incompetent, astray.

When we head
in one direction,
the pain goes away.

Within two layers of skin,
I sigh
like the primum mobile

or moving sculpture, oil and water,
enclosed on a coffee
table.

Aesculapius took my blood,
and my spirit
ran into the heavens. Yet,

here are my serpents!
I am 99%
de l'eau.

The rest, bowl.

The basis for friendship is
community of interest. Wolves
mate for life.

Yet they call our families "packs"
like decks of cards.
A communard who knows

how to have a good time with others,
I object to this moniker
of shuffling beast. It's true

that the only way to eat
is ultimately to rip something apart,
but you can't swallow

with your eyes, and besides,
we wolves have big hearts:
We are gentle, bright,

and penultimately kind.
Survival rules,
but after that comes conviviality!

A wolf attack on a moose
is no worse
than the conventions

of nations,
or the strategies
of most political parties.

It was a wall of panic that kept me away
from all that fancy language
and from the blind decay of society

where everybody respects memory and the Code.
They even called me Black Marten behind my back.
At night in my burrow I was sick.

Now the insanity has seeped into my glands.
Mephitic, my clan
warned me that nobody would care about a private world.
I should have flattered them

with how good they all smelled. They would have called n

"Pungent"
and placed me at their own sexual level.

In Polynesia,
they call me Iwa,

the frigate bird
filled with lice.

I nest
on the white-blossoming scaevola

bush. A cannibal, black
murderer.

I escort the boobies
out to sea

to rob them.
My throat turns blood red.

You are better off
if I stay fed.

Awakening
in an ancient teak,
in the dense forests
of the Siamese,

I smell the breath
of new plums
among the fulminating
odors of morning.

Then I plunge
into the maze of leaf
and bark, four arms.
At the end of my range,

like an inverted bowl:
the plum tree
steaming in the sun
with cold dew.

My natal chart
is of the bundle variety, meaning I must try
hard to relate.

Everybody asks me how I make love,
but then nobody wants to try it.

Then I get angry and swing my tail
around and everybody ducks.
I don't think they take me seriously.

I've tried to tell them,
I want them to know how I try
to be decent.
I want to be respected for what I am:

a cuddly little animal,
burdened with swords.

Every harvest our White One
is taken to the Island of the Sun
and sacrificed to Pacha Mama,
the Terrible One.

Then our blood seeps into the ground,
making the sunshine
flow like lava
smelling of new wine.

Above the Altiplano,
the clouds vibrate like metal tines
as our beating heart
is torn out of Its side

and laid on the ground
among bread and charmed flowers:
a great burden handed down
below the awesome, sympathetic towers.

Jeremiah said we cannot change.
I would like to get my jaws around Jeremiah,
and then we would see who can change faster.

At certain times I have dreamt

I tunneled under the ground
and looked for visionaries who were discarded many
years ago.

When I found them, I rescued them, let them see
the light then ate them.
More than one prophet of the Second Coming
have been surprised that way.

If the twenty-four buddhas were to wander under my tree,
discoursing on the Eightfold Path,

I would show them the instant teeth
of Maya.

I wear a necklace saying Noli Me Tangere,
but the yokels in Montana
don't understand. To them
I am nothing but venison: something to be shot
and jerked.

In my heart I know I have more going for me
than anybody who shoots me. I am gentle, fragile, kind;

the living evidence of man's superiority
over very little.

Poor man, who will never know
peace. Every year I throw my antlers away.

Once a rat climbed up Yggdrasil
looking for something precious, something vital.
Ten million years later he descended with ten acorns,
one for every possible sin,
transformed into a squirrel.

Since then, we have informed the forests like underbrush,
an all-American meal,
schizy, oversexed, plush,
with a message for the masses that keep America bestial:

In the mythic age, before the mast,
there was a god in the trees who liked to vote.
He was always confronted with choices, A and B,
taking the one that cost him least, others most.

Up in the boughs he called himself a democrat
and instructed our forefather hero, Demo-rat.

Blue
bulges to the surface of the tidewater
then runs

out into the middle of the bay
below the sun,
throwing vague messages back and forth
across, like a fine sand.

All that blue!
seeping into the shells
I should eventually crack to eat,

while I hear the
green cups of the sea waving their
snow teeth.

We explode,
our female

anodes
sending swarms

flying off like electrons
in a current

that electrolyzes plants.
Forming honey,

ant
money.

My forefathers grew out of a fish
that was torn apart. Even now,
when I see brutality,
it still smarts. But the sea is love.

I work it into my body where it mixes with ink.
There are poets who would love to feel like me:
to sow confusion in the wake of anything big.
My tentacles move crab up toward my beak like a machine.

I was once told that to study origins
we octopi would have to empty the ocean
so that every living being would either have to die
or change. Conclusion:

Wherever and regardless,
there is always some sort of sea
that forms in itself and unforms,
filled with the solid emotions of fish and stars.

I am a massive lichen, prone
to give off an odor when alone.

Dreaming through the grim decay of winter, a splinter,
under a log, waterlogged, a salamander,
never taking a gander at the cold outside,

not out of pride, but out of a desire not to get brittle
in January,
it is already past Groundhog Day when I emerge

and scoot down to the verge of the pond, jump in and swim.
Then it's a hassle looking for a mate:
We whirl in circles until fate decrees that she's for me,

and then I lay it on her, plenty of spermatic jelly
which she scoops up under her belly in a hole called a cloaca.
It is really nothing spectacular,

but then again it produces more of the same
strain
wrapped in a thick fluid. Later, out come little sticks

with gills and balancers but no legs. These grow afterwards.
If a creature is a good eater,
it will eventually develop lungs and crawl out of the water

and live on the border, where it will chew arthropods,
annelida, et cetera. And then when it turns cold it will shoot
back under another log

and descend into the fog
where God
sleeps like a spotted rod.

I survive
in the penumbral state

and thrive
on sunlit shade

where my chloroplasts,
slender, radiate

from a central point
and act

like a plant.
I participate

in the glory of heat,
but when push

comes to shove,
I'm out

on the lookout
for meat.

Over the pond the muskrats skitter
on ice, the brittle trees are rancid with the dead
buried underneath,
and in a branch a crow

haunted by memories of a hundred meals,
a hundred species of animal all dying
with a different cry from the seeds and berries. I
eat almost anything,
make any sound, fly anywhere, but will always be

black, dirty, cunning crow,
scheming for new food. This early spring scene is teeming
with its routine surge of life to be born. The deep cold
has come to the surface of the air
and broken apart,

and my heart
is looking to mate and build a platform in the trees
from which to survey the ripening of fruit
and the bursting of bodies.

Hercules had no need
to appease
my beheaded state

so that
the newly discovered form
would grow

from the tip of the toes
upward
or out of an egg when

carbon dioxide stands
in the way.
"I want to live,"

as Susan Hayward would say,
and shall be inventive
in order to stay:

A thread of life, I
tie pretty bows around my
paralyzed prey.

Inside the steppes of Asia, I create
my own steps to elevate
my crèche

and an escape hatch
from which to escape
when pressed.

Then I skitter across the plains,
fast as a horse, bounding away
on my two huge legs.

Like a shadow in the grass,
I chase down insects.
My tail

extends out like the end
of a kite. I am the shape of sand,
moving. Still, tripodal.

I am hardened
and can cut through space,
and leave little scars in the air
wherever I move my body.

I cover these up
with colors I schemed while lying in soup.

Once upon a time, an iguana spoke,
was stepped on,
and something pulled the inner lining of
his tail through his mouth,

so
there is nothing I can now do
which doesn't pare away at the somebody

I am about to become.

Underneath the sunshine and bright leaves,
the surface tension of the garden, a city,
millions of lives,
the bugs and beetles,
in the most vicious society imaginable.

The only protection here is reproduction,
a stream governed only by direction,
endless fodder,
aphids, larvae, caterpillars,
a mass of quivering guts and chitin,

and in their midst a mother
with her children on fire
who must get home:
a myth of compassion
in a sea of green, corrosive foam.

Good morning to the day and next my voles
buried under the hedge away from the stoats,
badgers, and other intellectual goats.

In my territory, I am the champ, using skill
to surpass all other animals, except hounds
and their field of nasty vermin,
who chase me over the grounds.

When I hear the word, "Tallyho," I go!
It's one hundred to one, so I try to splatter them
up against natural obstacles.

This earth is a paradise here on earth: home,
assiduously cleared of scat and bones,
where my vixen raises our children

and trains them to out-think
aristocrats and underlings.

A hideous green,
the color of digestion,

rises from the deep
when the sea calms.

A sack around what
contains it is me:

a comb jelly,
the ultimate

in animal simplicity.
O, sightless Form,

your endless eyes
can't lead the blind!

For sight itself
is nothing more

than a door
within a rind.

I was born into darkness, and from here I'll stray,
a worm's final plumage,
a breeding form of decay
unable to feed, merely an appendage,

the manifestation of an earlier manifestation's wish
for compulsive sadness.

Once I have laid my eggs,
I am useless and beyond the concept of health,
dreaming of light that can reverse my destruction:

white, virgin Light,
devoid of sex, devoid of death,
come to save me with bright, flaming tungsten.

Delicate and pink,
stately,

unique,
with an upside-down beak

hinged at the top,
when I take off,

the sky
absorbs my cast

and moves ever
slightly

toward the verge
of dusk.

Blistering white
with black spots of blood
scotched into my flesh,
my small eyes glistering like bullets,

manned and broken in the field
then strapped in a jess,
ready at the removal of the abyss
to plummet through space,

the sky stiffens like ice
and traps all other forms at slow speeds
whenever I sponsor my urges to proceed
on behalf of someone so deliberate:

my feudal master on the ground,
who loves to kill at a distance.

I am the siren whose loveliness called
the wracked bodies of seamen back
to the terrors of sexuality,

then revealed to them
the hideous exterior proportions of a cow
huddled with her baby.

For this they doomed me to slaughter,
picked apart my herd,
so that when I called, all I heard
were the agonies of fishermen,
the breathing of nylon nets and gunpowder explosions.

Now, the shallows of the Red Sea contain
nobody to love. When they haul me up on the beach
to dry me out,

my seduction is to cry.

The sun was black on our backs, and in the shade
below, the sounds of our males
were like the clanking of chains below the meadows.

We would come to rest from time to time
and clear the debris. We always left a morsel or two
for other insects, then rose to watch

the big ones run around in their hats,
helpless for lack of anyone large enough to shoot.
We'd taken away one of their years. Shit!
As if there could be more than one year for *us*.

Soon, they packed their bags and moved on,
unaware of their freedom. From the top,

it looked like a grey sea destroying
everything in its wake. I wish
there were a way to destroy their eggs;

I wish there were a place to land
away from the human race. Legend
has it that they originally came out of the East,

equipped with strange poisons and a god named Fred.

There is something about it
that lets
nothing enter it,

just attach.
Exclusive mass,
lasting,

which I slowly shape.
My radula scrapes
against the rim flakes,

creating change
with the steady drainage
of the tide pools, the same

art fosters.
Generations of pain lost
define our host.

Across the wastes I go.
On the horizon I see a mirage, a white bone
ringing like a tuning fork. My tribe

has cultivated an enlightened form:
the perfect nasty camel
who would walk a mile for a human being.

We have built a world of status in this desert based
on hump hair. The last winner
came from Karistan. I would say that our humor

precipitated off our skulls.

I would also lay claim to the title,
"Bearer of Genitals."
Living for forty years in emptiness,
one knows what it means to carry around a real burden.

Bereft of friends,
what makes us so durable in the sand? It is
this strange inability to be funny. We know

when the sands laugh, the drivers drop to their knees.

Specialty presumes
the ability to transcend or else resolves itself
into function. I could do

something different given a new
leg or circumstance
from which my requirements grew.

Here below,
everything is suited toward an end
that never comes.

I move out looking for scraps;
durable but digestible,
I am programmed to fashion my world

into a tiny map.

Whether natural or mutation,
there is no effective simulation

for disembowelment,
except a factitious garment.

A wolf in sheep's clothing
inspires a justifiable loathing

in the sheep. I can envision
a spring collection made from human skin

for giants: From white to black,
sized and fumigated on a rack,

they would have to remove the musk and small hairs,
apply some baby oil in drier weather.

The price would be quite low
for unstripped pelts,

since the insides are worthless
yet always up for sale.

Why is it all so tiny,
so backward,
that I was stuffed inside my mother here

in a hurry,
a furry flurry, whereas
in Mongolia

the ground moves so slowly
it takes only a few gerbils
to keep up with it?

Sweet and trim,
a diversion
in new form that has filled

the bedrooms
of nine-year-old girls
since 1954,

in Latin I mean
Persian warrior-god wearing battle helmet tusks cut
from boar.

In garbage I can always find
something to be washed and retrieved:
a bone that's barely good enough,
some hamburger with bacon grease.

Society has forged its rules,
intent on such frugality
that what remains of the ancient wild
is meager and unsanitary.

What was it that forced me by the head down
into darkness
where we all dig the same sane web?

Perhaps it was something large that escaped
my senses and created my food.
Perhaps it was something that stood
in front of the sun and created my first mood.

There is a hunger that will never give way:
No matter how far I tunnel, it follows behind me
with its thick tongue.

Ahead I hear grubs writhing
in anticipated pain, in the Medium.

I will keep on moving through this feast
until one day
the feast moves through me or my tunnel ends,

delicately balanced at the edge of the universe
between two flames.

After the seventh year,
I appeared
and stayed,

but nobody knew
because
discovery

meant
that the truth
would be hidden

by death.
Experience was compacted
into

nothing.
Now I've devolved
into

a lizard —
experienced
as something.

The difference is
sensation
lives.

They bred me out of a jack
and into a mare,
but there is no real need for anybody to stare
at me. After all, soon all the races will fall

into a tube to grate
against the walls for the side of a womb.
Then the whole biological process will tumble into the hand
of boobs with their clones, their genetic programming
and frozen sperm.

You would kick somebody, too,
if you were continually splitting in two,
invisibly. A team with twenty mules truly has
forty.

My song is definition,
conclusive and precise.
Rhetoric, erudition
and sentimentality

I leave to other poets,
whose language,
as we know it,
does vague damage.

In the sky,
flocks of delicate beings
float by,
expressing their feelings

in the soughing of egos
they call "the wind."
They have no control,
no taste, no judgment;

while deep in the forest
my message is relaxed and clear,
impressed
in a magic mirror where

beauty and pain
reflect
again and again and again
the same bottomless defect.

Above the horizon there seems to be a point
where nobody else can see. There stands
a demon with a funnel to collect the sun.

We teach our children never to look in that direction.

The trees sway full of fruit and leaves, full of breezes
to fan us when we're sad. We are the gentle camelopards,
reticulated but simple, never bad to anybody. When

we get mad, we spar with our brains
at the tips of our swords. It's tough to get hurt.
Even if we wanted, it is almost impossible to bite
the dirt.

There are birds that run up and down our necks
and some
fly in circles around our heads. They know how they got
their wings but ask

how our necks got long. Little do they know
that our bodies floated down toward the ground
while we refused to give away our view. In the East
we see

an angel with rainbow wings and full of heat
every morning create a new sun.

Here I am
eagerly waiting
for a huge blob
to bomb. Then:

Tenno Heika Banzai!
If I miss,
I just climb up
and try again.

Once on,
my beak goes in,
and it's unlimited
cherry phosphate

unless I get zapped
with a match,
tweezers or gas.
But best of all,

there are always
more soldiers
where I come from
ready to fall.

$CaCO_3$

waves in the breeze;
my pedicellariae feast.

Each spine is anchored
to the movement of a star,
controlling the destiny
burning

inside my lantern.

I am a creature
of the universe, but at the center.
Integral,

when I eat,
somewhere far away the lights dim.

Like most poets,
I eat my mother's scat
while snug in her pocket.

Success based on cuteness,
they say my soul is
a child dead and restless

to return.
(Poet's yearn
for a child's scorn

of refined knowledge
picked up in your better colleges.
Better to garbage

up writing with vanity and insanity!)
My cupidity is for cough remedies
made in heaven. Oh, lucidity

is even within my animal range.
I am pretty little teddy displaying
sensitivity, a grunge playing

on the moral conscience of Australia.
There is better paraphernalia
in any opera seria.

Better to eat diarrhea
than engage in onomatopoeia.
Just another idea.

The world spins, twirls,
beyond my misery
trapped in the barrel
of my skin.

My reddish hair
thinning down with years
under my square shoulders,
permanent tears

invisible on my clown
face burn.
I was made as a stage
to higher intelligence.

Just one step beyond, man:
no longer able to climb,
no more able to cope,
sensitive and impotent.

Why would anybody
give up the sky

for the dark forest floor
at night?

The answer lies
within my bones

which gathered heaviness
for reasons of their own.

My grandfather told me I
was one of the oldest living creatures.

I remember seeing him
frozen in an ice cube. All he could do was wink.
I dream about it whenever I move through something grey.

One of my brothers died from cleaning himself
with borax. Another screamed for help from inside
a wide-mouthed jar. There was nothing we could do.

At night when I come out of the wall,
I am drawn by a desire for something dirty.
Something white, shiny, and filthy

like the light from the sun.

When we are together,
almost nothing can separate us:
only the spirits which tempt us
toward the graveyards.

We care about each other.
I've seen one toothache
drive our whole herd wild. And every moment
a world of compassion enters our scent
and changes into color.

What does it mean to be tame?
That dazed look that inhabits our brothers
like a brittle flame
as they watch us being driven into the pens.

When love makes us strong,
no one has ever seen us raise
our trunks in the air to make the sunrise blaze

or bring back our ancestors to sing old songs
that protect our children from malice
and from the darkness of the circus.

In color and aragonite
I splay, creating underneath me
the sights
of the fabulous, breathing reef,

where at night we emerge,
purple, red, green, yellow and tan—
with gramma, beau gregory and grouper;
their hypnotic eyes, our poison wands—

to captivate, secrete and grow.
We are the final barrier.
Upon our jeweled thrones are thrown
the nameless, shorn of terror.

Man in his ultimate wisdom forbade
that his own food be used. I graze
alongside starving children.

Desire, sayeth the Gita, is our enemy.

Better a fat cow
and a dead baby.

Living long, I carry
unincorporated voices,

quintessential remarks
of spirits now buried,

whose dreams were drawn
onto my gnarled tongue,

then parodied. For
language is simply a form,

the mimic of a world once flesh
and holy, but grammatically

deformed. The dead resolve
in my cage; their hellos

and pleas for food now stripped
of all personal rage.

Whenever the phone rang, the mouse
ran into the wall.
He was more afraid of bugs than he was of cats.

This mouse ate cheese like everyone else,
but he feared what cheese would do to his system.
Between the rapid beats of his heart there was

a deathly silence.

I feel that his pelt would make a nice coat
and wonder who would wear it.
Maybe it would be a series of mice

or a large rodent like myself
who looks like a mouse.

Down the egg tube I tumbled, gathering shell.
Within days I looked like a human
til the beak came out to tell me I'd be dumb.

All that growth: eggs for breakfast
three times a day. Wow! And then the hectic scramble
to get out, I emerged into the night life
of the coop surrounded by coils and wire.

Several days later we were inoculated in billows.
We piled up against the fences; random chicks
were flattened against the bottom. Too bad!
Then there were several weak ones that we pecked
apart. What fun!!

Time passed, until I debuted. Plump, theoretically nutritiou
I was nominated the King of the Roost.

Now on bright mornings I crow
how we birds one day will soar over the graves of men,
over their farms, over the last take-out stands,

and how the human race will eventually descend
to the intellectual and aesthetic level
of barnyard chickens.

Beneath the waves,
Above the ocean floor,
Revolving,
Revolving,
A serrated sword
Cuts
Under the brave
Diver,
And it's all over.

My skin filled with tumors, and my thoughts
were already heading downstream
when I stooped over the redd and let go.

The milt seeped down like starlight over the desert.
It was cold and pure like this haven.
It was quiet and satisfying.

I remember the ordeal
through the sewers and through the nets;
I remember the raccoons crashing
through the rocks, beheading lifelong friends.
I remember many years ago watching
as this struggle unfolded in my yolk.

Now I'll float.

This must have been some mechanism of the heart.
There was no reason for what I did

and no name for the light in the water
that told me to return.

I hover
over my egg held between my knees,
a man among men,
unloved.

For sixty days,
through the long winter, fasting and waiting
for children,
the temperature drops toward zero Kelvin,

and our bones rot in the snow straining.
Our eyes are closed.
It is like a white mass thrown
down: faceless purity,

vicious and yet totally empty,
what we must survive
in order to reproduce and thrive;
form without content,

at the edge of a continent,
where the days fly
like flat grains
across a lens,

eventually breaking
with the heavy pounding

of breath and light.

Whether Marsh Rabbit or Hudson Seal,
these are simply words to make me seem
palatable and palpable.

I don't look so hot,
especially when I am swimming in a bog
or sunning, putrid, on a log,

but I get the job done and survive.
In the winter I live
under the ice. I like it
nice and wet so that I can thrive.

The inhabitants of this island
are becoming fewer and fewer.
But I can raise my litter

in any garden variety of sewer.
I am a winner

among spectacular losers.

My bird's head pecks at anything
it can get, leaving
destruction. It can't swallow, is separate,
simply a head.

My worm body writhes in a cage,
cannot excrete and quickly dies, is eaten then
by the cage.

My cradle eats the body then secretes
another body, again to grow and die while the bird pecks.

And meantime the lace forms, moving out and out
over the rock. A mat.

I will do almost anything short of stupidity
to defend my nest.
I can't move my eyes around,
but I have a neck so it doesn't matter.

Who? Who?

The answer to this universal question is
me.

I'm not a common goatsucker, you know.

Men think me wise, and by their standards
I am:

Quiet and vicious,
I vomit up the bones of rats.

After one year I
have emerged pure,

having left all of my fears
awash
in another world,

to rise into the air
awing,
to make love delighted in a way
no one can ever again be.

Grappling
with another doomed infant,
I'm so small, so inconsequential,

yet so free.

Once as a brock I was all set
to turn a terrier into a wet red blanket
when it bolted. If it had stayed around,

I would have been dug out of the ground with tongs.
Now as an adult I rip apart
the homes of small animals with my claws:

Badger: Knock knock.
Vole: Who's there?
Badger: Badger.
Vole: Badger who?

Badger: Badger gonna vole very sick.
That vole didn't appreciate my humor

one lick.

Among the eelgrass and sargassum,
there is a knight that plays possum: seahorse, me,
one of the most bizarre animals in the sea.
With four rotary blades I clumsily maneuver,
and my mouth works like a hoover.

My children are shot into the water by males
who carry them in pouches over their tails.
When we want to be noticed, we snap our necks: click!
click! click!
With protective coloration we play our tricks

on anything big that likes to eat
someone erect, goggle-eyed, eccentric and discrete.
I am the seahorse, a tiny
anomaly.

The charm comes about
in a moment
as an act of defense.

Up I go,
absurdly spread out,
filled with venom
and innocence.

It is possible
that this man
could do some damage,

kill me like a mongoose.
Around my wicker
house,

there is something
in the air,

something beyond
my four senses,
rising with the dust.

I am the curse
that slits air,

spilling blood
on wayfarers lost

between the coasts
when there's no wind,

so that, then,
I am incapable

of being what I've been.
Yet only a few can

understand
the gist

of this predicament
and watch

the sky fall
into the ocean

like red rain,
scarlet petals

settling like coals
on the brain.

Dashing over the prairie,
smashing air

like a giant wheel,
crushing small sheets of foam
hanging in the light,

and at night, all alone,
gathering lost speed
back into my knees,

I am the cinnamon pronghorn,
whose pompons are hidden
behind white rosettes

as I fly
into a new dimension, a compartment, a blind
of streaming tinsel,
where time

is motionless.

On our own scale
we are as beautiful
and diverse
as any possible universe:

sublimely eccentric,
Rube Goldberg life;
parthenogenic
and capable of resurrection;

spoke-headed, cement-toed,
whose males have no powers
of digestion,
simply floating penises

capable of hypodermic
injections of sperm;
others resemble worms
(but we all have wheels).

You'll find us in your gutters
or within your next meal:
an invisible dimension
ruled by invention.

Sixty million of us stood exposed on the plains,
waiting for the knives and bullets
that would lay us away.

Our only solace was
we knew all those Indians would go with us.
They wandered drunk
through the herds, slashing at our stomachs.

The Whites, on the other hand,
placed their stands downwind and then piled our skulls up
against their outhouses
until enough heads were accumulated to ship away
for bone charcoal.

They killed so many of our kind
it raised the topsoil
above the level of the Indians.

A wingless bat with
Fu Manchu fingers,

driven out of Madagascar
by real estate developers,

"Nay-nay,"
I say when asked

about the future.
There will be none.

I am the most primitive primate.
It was fun.

I run parallel to the ground
so that the sound
of my crusty legs vibrates

into the air in conforming
rays and my "x"'s
pound

into the soil,
taking
their toll of rattlesnakes.

My cobalt crest
puffs
when anger mounts

from out of nowhere.
And my cry
resounds.

It is like
a stick on a picket
fence or a dove

rattling.
It is the cry
of competence

battling dryness,
necessity
tempered by wryness.

I am the wisest animal.
I always stayed in the most important sense
right where I am.

At one time or another,
everybody specialized and went the wrong way, developing
useless heads and arms to be
waved in the distance.

(A shark can bite off an arm,
but I simply make its teeth dirty.)

Where there is no night and day,
I move through a universe of shimmering particles,
eating.

I have never died
and never will.

Every time I split, I say good-bye to my eternal self.

Damp and neglected,
they stand on their shelves
like soldiers, ready to be delved.

Their war is not mine.
This nebulous battle against obscurity
is a form of heredity

once removed: lives forsaken
in an inoffensive campaign toward some truth
that generates mass infestations of mildew.

What has been gained? A little space.
The words are knitted together like small bones
over skin. Bloodless halftones; all urgency gone,

the battle lost to sickness
before it could be won. And the trick was accuracy—
simply to define the disease.

Now I feed.
These books have no means of defense
unread. Only a fruitful and appalling innocence.

Like all the other animals,
I struggle with my memory.
I gave birth to something about seven months ago.

It wobbled around,
and then they led it away with a rope, muttering
about sweetbreads.

Once again, later on,
they took away those of us who wore
a different badge, who never came back.

I am a Holstein.
Because of my race, they feed me molasses and clover.

Today they gave me a dose of stilbestrol.
Tomorrow they are going to ship me to paradise
in a car

once reserved for Jews.

I was made
to make new

snow look
more beautiful.

It must have been my mineral-blue,
life-force preservative
that got me through,

so that my Crossopterygian brother,
Rhipidistian, could crawl
out of the water
and later catch me in a net.

I've lived
because my evolutionary
vacuole couldn't be punctured

while others' holes dissolved
into bad bets.

There go their bodies now!
Stratocumulus hovering over the sea,
darkening out of innocence

to reform into
doomed meat.

Instead of lagomorphs
you would think I preyed
on the seven dwarfs the way

I am trapped
with bombs, guns and getters.
There has to be a last resort, a better

method of survival.
I live
because my rivals' wits are hived

with inefficiency and greed.
One has to be patient,
cunning, feed with intelligence,

not "consume"
as the final equation
in a ruinous economy plagued by inflation.

When every individual is free
and self-sufficient,
efficiency destroys the organizations

which make men miserly
and mean.
My howl of ecstasy under the moon

is proof
that happiness
is not a roof, nor a full freezer chest.

Trillions of us thrips inhabit the planet
and, cell by cell, eat it.

On the fields of algae, within the dark swarms
of termites, in fungus, rose and lupine,

wherever there is life to be punctured, we are,
unrecognized, beyond control, raising scars.

The thrips know something men don't know.
There is only one form of superiority:

numerical.

Here in majestic solitude,
beyond the reach of man and wolf,
where ice-caps glisten with the Truth,
crystal and immovable,

violent winds enwrap our pain
and hurl it up the slate slopes
to vanish into history,
the azure vision of a ghost—

a world devoid of fear and growth
that dazzles, helpless, in the sun,
where all we meant and all we knew
has hardened, faceless and serene.

My flat head sticks
out of a tree,
my tail picking up

the leaves' subtle green,
a small hook to my bill
and to my voice:

now a whistle,
now a door squeaking,
now a waterfall of sound

leaking into a pool
of imbecility.
And my black eyes flash

a piercing white
when the devil inside me
shrieks at the light.

Pale green, with streaks of rosé,
I spend my days among white waters,
cold and frothy,

darting around. Only
my eyes detect mayflies, stone flies
above the spray.

The song of the brook began in the sky!
It moved through the ground then crystallized
in a liquid light that hypnotizes prey

to sink into my world
of clear motion; while far away
the clouds slide shadows across my scales.

Brook, clouds and trout,
alive and perfect,
are shimmering in a bottomless pail.

When God pulled out His giant easel,
He said, "I'm going to make Me a weasel.

A tubular animal with a nondescript palate
is suitable to My particular palette:

someone who derives pleasure from pain,
a sly and smelly and slightly insane

ermine, whose greatest value is his coat. Alas,
with what shall I fill the rest of My canvas?

Something half-eaten, fluttering in horror,
will yield to the efforts of a future Restorer

who will cover the bestiality of My creation
with cleverness and crucifixion."

So that is the story of my genesis
and how I came to work for Jesus.

I am the snowy egret,
egressing from regret,
from the swamp

where my parents were shot by hunters
then left to stink the mire,
floating with their feathers ripped from their backs.

I almost starved.

Yet now I'm back
flashing in the sun
that I have another purpose beside plumes

that plumb the depths of sky
for the white quintessence of blue.

I rise into the air,
an adornment
beyond the violence and degradation
of human truths.

A piece of kinetic sculpture in a dry land,
handless,
with only a few toes,
a scrawny neck and massive beak,

that punts its enemies when the odds are bleak
or else runs faster than a car,
is me, the great bird,

whose plumes are prized for hats and fans
by women with eyes similar to mine,
whose favorite word, "divine!" is continually taken
out of context. When I get up and go,

I am your typical extant animal
going extinct: whose feet are fast
but whose brain is slow;

whose value
in the scheme of man and womankind is to be viewed.
I am the bird whose friends hide in the ground
where I dive

to escape the eternal ugliness that created me,
then plucked me and shucked me.

Above our dorm,
everybody is expected to perform,
dream,

or at best totally
rest. We simply riddle
the collective unconscious

with our pygmy
invasion. The darkest
fantasies are surrounded

by a vulnerable
surface.

Here I am, first in war and first in peace,
but as far as first in my country is concerned,
I would rather be sunning in Nice.

Still, I shall remain at the top of the list
unless Alvar Aalto is declared a fish.

With my ears and tail like ripe bananas,
I roam the nocturnal savannahs after termites,
whom I love to see stripe
my tongue,

while when faced with a lion
I lower myself into the ground.
This profound method protects me, and always will,
until some day

those lions lose their fear of creatures
hunched in graves.

Making love is private.
It is the most private

act in the world.
Closed off,

two bodies tell each other
how much they always hurt.

Come each Second of February,
my image moves out of the ground
and takes me over, and changes the weather.

A ghost, it rises up to haunt me:
a black vestige of winter
with its own inner logic that moves inward.

For the past three months
I've led a different life, motionless,
while my mind hashed at the snow

with small knives and my spine
moved around some pole.
Sleep, slow dissolution in harmony,

out to get me in the form of a shadow,
now bends its tiny ears
across the silent meadow.

Up in the northern wilds stands a tree
tinseled with frail bodies impaled on twigs:
frozen birds, mice dangling from the knees.

A tree in winter with bodies for leaves,

and nearby the decorator . . . .

Hovering, waiting,
anticipating; always ready to kill more than I can eat;
butcherbird, mass murderer, thrill killer.

Just for fun I'll rip off a head
or break a spine with my beak. When hungry,
I'll eat an animal whole and shit out the bones.

I am the cleaver and decimator,
whose vision (like the human politicians')

is to fill the world with cadavers.

Protozoa and hormones combine
within my delicate structure to refine cellulose
and make me fierce:
a soldier with a point of view
directed toward ants and toward aardvarks, too.

I had a nightmare. A river flowed to the sea.
Within the estuary stood a tree,
and inside was me,
running in circles around Queenie, who was swollen
up like a box.

I remember also how a voice rode along the water,
telling me the name of a womb
that could give birth to anything!

Now, awake in the dark, I take a moist breath while
Queenie continues her grunting.

On the margins of the land, I stand
not very high: a dragon, with a vice
not much different from a vise
to separate an animal's feet from its hands.

My osteoderms sparkle on the bags
and shoes of parvenus. My teeth
were used by horny Romans as charmed tokens.
I have always been a fount of superstition,

a symbol of fertility and perdition.
When I snap, my prey goes zap
and empties itself of all mental divisions.

Feral and dull,
we primp and strut through the garbage of Metropolis.
Green, purple and grey like vomit,

ugly birds, unlike our relatives who rediscovered the dry world,
we have become intergraded like Norwegian rats
into the worst world of them all:

the urban vat.
Our cousins, the Passengers, were cleared with the forests
to make way for new flocks with their iron forests;

the city,
where the primary human emotions are confusion and self-pity,
is our endomorphic home.

There, at dawn,
we deliver our guano like sour milk
downward to darkness on extended wings of filth.

At night, I emerge,
rare and lonely.
Civilization has pursued me
up the Cordillera;

there are only one hundred
of us left. Browsing
in a cold Andean stream,
in the riffle of the lights

I see my ancestors
shepherd the dead
toward distant lakes of fire.

Fastest of all birds, my ancestors
decided to nest on top of humans, unawares.
This almost banished fear

from our repertoire.
I was born
on a bright morning

stuck to a black wall.
Later I fell.
I remember climbing back up the tunnel,

screaming for Mother. Brick by coated brick,
I labored up the stack, cold and sick
and needing to be reborn. I made it.

Now, light in the air, I scramble so high,
I am practically out of sight,
covering as many as five hundred miles before nightfall

brings me back to the hearth
with top-speed, delicate machinery. The earth
will claim me only when my heart

unleashes this terrible clamor of efficiency
and settles like a leaf
down into its own chimney.

It's tough to be born
to take orders and to be
underneath someone's rectum all day,

yet a subtle betrayal of nature
made me fit for this
by making me swift.

My uncle, a Great Shire,
once told me there was nothing
to the hearts of men.

Beside a wall scribbled
with horseblood,
he died in a factory.

Gentle Rider, there is a better
land for You and me:
on the other side of the clouds,

a pink meadow,
where we shall gallop wild
through the darkening billows

of sunset. Your power
so light on my mouth.
Your paths: a perfect home.

Moving downstream,
heading for the Sargasso Sea,
other mothers

are also heading there,
ready to die after breeding.
Soon each will release

twenty million children,
small leaves to return
back up the branches,

the rivers of two continents
embedded in flesh.

Here I,
a marginal animal always on the periphery of sight,
am on shelves, under tables.

Over the years,
we entered the world of the box, an atmosphere
of residential delights and tears.

I keep a wall jammed
between myself and others. Slobbering humans!
I would rather be plundering

in the jungle
than licking chopped liver from cans.
Domestic felicity,

perversion surrounded by privacy,
is a blatant contradiction that has trapped me
in this kitchen:

reductio ad absurdum man,
listening for the sound of his doorbell, pressed
by an ill wind.

Trudging across the land,
I glide on a bed of my own spit.
Without spite, I try my hand
at getting a better grasp

on the path. The future lies
always before my eyes,
and the past is always
behind me, a burden

lodged in a protective cast,
never to be removed.
Time and I relentless
in the same messy groove.

Yet my shell is ornamental,
for when I toss it in,
I won't become a corpse,
I'll become a coffin!

And therefore I am proof
that strife empties
at the end of life.
All else is saliva and fiction.

Not even an earthquake can kill a worm
the way a robin can.
If I keep my head on, though,
I still have half a chance.

Underneath the ground,
I've spent aeons searching for my eyes,
but after all the other forms of sight have disappeared
on top, I'll still be down here looking, blind.

When an animal is buried, it gives me especial delight
being thrust deep where all I can hear is its fear.
Men fight wars underground.

We worms like to huddle around and listen
before we attack.

In every home there exists
the possibility
of cancer:

of a child who grows too fast,
of a tumor
dominating the nest.

Other children will wane and die,
starving, while I
watch amused from my perch

on the hide of a cow.
Rosemary's baby is grabbing
all the food!

And soon she'll fly
from her confused stepmother,
left grinding

shell, eye and feather
into the nest's
absorbent lining.

Regal, sanguine, generous me.
My bounty extends across the savannah
in little red piles—provender for hyenas,
dogs, vultures and crocodiles.

Day and night I oversee
a life and death struggle for territory
and energy to breed.

Tribal love, protection of the young, courage in senility,
daring and speed are rendered in saliva:
wildebeest, zebra, gazelle, impala.

For in my court reigns Fate,
crowned by ritual slaughter,
which neither I nor my vassals dare
tergiversate.

Flying out of my northern
havens
(which I shall refuse to rhyme
herein

with the word "raven,"
since I've been tormented
over and over

by "Nevermore,"

a homonym,
a mythical city by the sea

overlooking Oakland,
where no bird has ever been
without a loss of value),

I arrived
at the Land of American Poetry,
a dark land devoid of meaning,

where I perched,
hunched among blacknesses
that were crawling in search
of each other's

addresses.

Life is not a dream

but a real-life lepidoptera
with problems making a living.

Some believe
that what happens in the chrysalis is miraculous
as if there were a spirit who hops
between two animals!

But I remember how, in my own world,
the delusions reformed
like the movement of railroad ties. So painful and terrible.

40,000 eyes; feelers
reflecting waves of sensation; nectar; scales
vibrating in the cold spring breeze.
Underneath the glamor, it was all

an empty routine.
Vanity.

Old Chuang Tzu once dreamt he was a butterfly,
then wondered
if the butterfly were now dreaming he was him.

Overhead the sky is forever changing
and covers all dreams. There is nothing here with a conscien
that doesn't eat

out of the same miserable lunchbucket.

Supported on all six sides by air, and my wings
moving rhythmically in six directions
as I rest,

I think on what inside me makes me be
what I am: a rainbow bird frozen
with foreboding.

How I glide
from side to side,
sucking out the scarlet runner bean and columbine
while my thoughts rage under the sun
and in the breeze.

This garden quivers
with warmth and prosperity.
Every petal, every leaf, is active and free.

The branches overhead swell with ease!

Yet the pleasures in all that I know
have dissolved into a dull, steady hum,
an aureole,

my sadness so painful and so completely
divorced from relief; it is the impossibility of being
something acceptable;
defeat,

which gave me the power to be,
will one day reclaim its portion, blossom out
and paralyze me.

There is no reason
why suction
should not play its part
in art

by guiding men
within those infinite
vacuums
and exhalations

of literary
criticism. There,
after the first swirl
of wind,

one would taste
satisfaction
in a red paste:
nutrition

flowing in the veins,
containing
somebody else's loss,
discrete and unseen.

Great art is based
on restraint.
Wrapping the subject
in magic chains.

Not a flicker
of self-indulgence
must be allowed
and no inflation.

Poison
must not affect the one
who cradles poisons.
Emotion

must not affect
the precision of motion.
The subject
must be apprehensible

and in need.
Great art is based
on restraint, content, grace
and certainty.

A dark mist whipped against the skerries.
The moon revolved around the Pole.
The last of our calves scurried
across the thickening ice for the polynyas.

A rapid freeze, almost as bad as the harpoons
of Little Diomede, when our skins
were nailed up along the strait,
it was death to think of hesitating.

Farther south, we knew, the diapason
of the broad water would welcome us.
Now we linger in its volume
of essential calm: beyond seasons, migrations,

beyond life hurrying to subsume
another form, tumbling before another broom.

I am the winged medium between the dead and heaven.
Anybody who wants to get there has to pay
the price of admission: to become rotten.
If you are visible, you can rise in less than three days!

I lay my eggs in protected spaces without a nest.
My bad breath is more than enough protection.
When I look in your direction,
it is easy to lose your appetite for omelettes.

Floating in the sky, the very last
to land and feed, when I'm done,
it's as if no one had ever been taken to task!
Creature, if you are someone

who wants to survive after death,
skip the damp earth with its funereal pomposities.
Reemerge in my form, soar, and feast
on whoever is left.

Far from the ancient coign
of Greece,
I sparkle in realms
of fantasy

where I prey on the nerves
of certain
men and women. Some would say "flash in
the pan"

in order properly to designate
my effect.
I am the deep frustration
of sex.

Red, white, blue and black,
I stagger
on the periphery of inaction;
my thighs

tremble in snow and moist heat.
I appear
wherever axon and dendrite barely agree
to meet.

Like all beetles,
divided in three,
sheath winged,

on the surface
of the water we swing
round and round

on bubbles,
looking for a foundering
insect in trouble.

Then, as a pack,
we strike at once
and tear our prey

apart,
waiting for its
silence, as the foam

covers the quivering
parts.
Simply speckles

causing ripples,
a slight disturbance
or transverse movement,

we are such cute
phenomena:
Brownian piranhas.

Mass of life,
forming small balls
inside,

the world around
is no more profound
than that within.

My friends call me "Blob."
I grow and I throb.
My food can be seen

internally,
although my moods
stay hidden.

I am the tiger, what you fear,
an embodiment of the shame that you feel.

When I kill, it is beautiful and graceful.
You cannot be me, and you're lucky
if I'll let you be at all.

You cannot afford self-respect
when I fall on your back! Surrender.
My claws

were forged in the fire of a great God
Who made you and the lamb with less love.

Within the order Acrasiales
there are three families:
Sappiniaceae, Guttulinaceae
and Dictyosteliaceae.

I am Dictyostelium Discoideum,
a slime mold,
a microbiological lump of gold

that aggregates on agar plates.
If you can pronounce me,
you probably know how to trounce me

with paraffin and take a section,
watch me become an erection
every fourth day, preceding soral ejection

into a morphogenetic pool,
like stippling moving alongside a canoe,
slurp down bacteria with gusto
and then reform into another pseudoplasmodial truss. O,

there is no science that can ever explain
my kinship with mankind, how my dimension
allows me to spread out and be: the unsolvable mystery
of collusion between mind and medium. Inexpressibly,

I condense, grex, invert, stretch, burst,
cast through space, feeding, recondense

then redisperse,
as valid, as awesome as the universe!

Snorting in peace and desolation
where fir and aspen grow like stalagmites,
obscuring the horizon,
I stagger beyond defense, aged and ripe.

My sexuality hangs its weathered bell
and swells in response to the season. Fall.
I strop my ancient velvet and below. Astounded,
the sullen woods resound.

My torn energy extends its train
of darkness, sinking back into the brain,
arousing images with torturous continuity
of wolves' ravening, yellow, infective teeth.

I stumble through the brush.
If only this vibration would cease. . . .
A red bubble rises in my voice
and empties slowly into the waiting forest.

Across the tops of the trees, I hear
the wallaroos
priding themselves on having become
a higher form of life not unmuch like us.

Inside my pocket Joey groans and tosses: my kid

who wants to live in the hills like the wallies and leap
across chasms. He would refrain from killing
blossoming plants
and would wipe Australia clean of all maleficence.

Life is an accumulation of possibilities which we
must weed, he said. (This child has abilities
not seen in the human world
since the birth of Pontius Pilate.)

This island is our evolutionary niche.

Here God is somewhere
near the top of the ladder, he added.
But even God is surrounded
by water.

What a dizzying leap of faith!
What progeny!

This child will grow to springboard
past the dons
who dominate the Marsupial Academy.

Deep in my body, there are little bones
that used to be feet. They resonate
whenever I come in sight of land.

With my tiny nose, ears and eyes,
I can hardly smell, hear or see.

I remember the first time I ran into the water,
afraid of everything but growth,
how my insides hollowed out, expanded,
as my nostrils sank below the foam.

Last winter I went south to the Blue Bay
with my baby. On the way,
she was eaten by a fish with teeth
the size of hatchets.

Now I lie at the bottom of the world,
under the watery mass of the world,
holding my breath,

terrified that the flensers will find me
and tear me apart.

Legend has it
that we feed

our children
in a pinch

by rending our breasts
for blood,

and this has made us
a symbol

of selfless motherhood.
Fine. But the truth of the matter is,

there is
no real substitute for

regurgitated
fish.

When I first climbed out of my burrow, I knew
I would never be troubled by forethought.

The sun soared through the air,
but I would never know where it was going,
and wouldn't care. *Innocence.*

When it rained, each drop came as a surprise.
Everything was right where it belonged;
everything was right in front of my eyes
except for my body, which also knew what to do.

Part of the order of things, I mumbled to myself
as I was preparing my ninth litter.
These children are part of some greater, better order.

And then I turned my pink eyes
toward the weightless blue.
A voice came down from on high, thundering:

Thank you, Rabbit,
for all that delicious food.

Nobody told me
I was in the midst of miracles

when I hit the sand, and
I don't believe it.

As if consciousness
could descend to criticize itself.
I am what I am:
a seal descendant

of a large bull
who held his ground and a small cow
who swam across the ocean
to be with me now.

To feed me between swims.

One day soon,
I shall leave to cavort
alone among the southern waves:

an ecstatic baby

at the pellucid edge
of foam.

Si-Ling-Shi, so beautiful,
your eyes in the garden
like small fruit seen through the mulberry,

sipping your tea,
dreaming of new forms of luxury
to satisfy

those delicate needs,

Si-Ling-Shi, Empress,
where is your subtlety now?

Spun through the sordid factories
that clothe the world.

Mascot for the state of blond brains,
I am busy building fossorial drains,
Safe from animals who would love to taste
My skin and bones in a bland paste.

I love to work, and I love to save
Each tuber and root that comes my way,
To drag it down by means of my pockets
Into my cellars, where I lock it.

No other gopher is of any importance,
Except for my wife who could be "Hortense."
I see her approximately twice a year
When my prick gets hard and the coast is clear.

Otherwise, I'm moving like a tan enema
Somewhere between Canada and the Isthmus of Panama.

Morning mist
rolls along the surface
of the lake,

far north
where the wind is
a soft breath

of desire
for a clear day.
The pines await
my echo,

a bodiless form
shattered by the light,

a loon sound
screaming for a loon
through the cold,

resistant quiet.

In the damp recesses of the cupboard,
I am searching for Her: my ideal

Beatrice among the silverfish,
young, delicate, to join me for a dance;

in a hush among the skillets
She will pick up my sperm packet,

and Love, that began in the still
depths of the ocean, will flood the kitchen.

The problem was
that everything ends.

This was the reason
they couldn't love endlessly.

It's not our fault! they complained.
Our lovers die, leave, change.

Every new leaf is an insult
to our love of the tree.

Every new cloud punctures
our sensibility. It's too free.

What we need is constancy,
probity, spontaneous joy

where change and love mix.
The shepherd responded,

Love is deep, endless sleep
where forms emerge to form dreams:

one after another,
the subjects of love. Always on the move.

You are love.
That will never change.

When they finally took the subject up,
they didn't know. The shepherd came along

and tried to describe the feeling for them.
It is not the urge to reproduce, just, he said.

His gaze was inward as if on something
that didn't matter but shone. Nor simply

the relationship of parts, nor of growth
and death, he said. His head was hardly moving.

It is nothing, less than nothing. Truly
less than nothing. Nothing has no beauty.

It is too much. Beauty is much smaller.
Between the animals and the smallest possible thing.

A man in his thirties came along.
He said, My entire life I was burdened

with structures and a sense of death.
My insides were never good enough.

Today, it all burned away and I wandered
here. Among a shepherd and my peers.

Now life shall flow around me, colorful,
sensitive, unmeaning. This emptiness

is totally revealing, the pleasures
entirely new in a new world. Sharp, true.

Melancholy paints the higher reaches
of air. I breathe the pain and lack of happiness,

aware that every thing and action possesses
sweetness. The animals were staring.

Glad to have you join the group, they said.
Take off your clothes and come live with us.

Worm and plant; bird and tree;
man and man.

Bug and fruit; fish and sea;
amoebae.

All were close: hugging, digging,
eating. Breathing.

The shepherd declared:
Like air and water,

we interpenetrate and free up
all that we know

in order to be close.
Importance is concentrated in touch.

The truth approaches
with parched lips; we caress

the dryness, feel moisture
burst forth in a primal kiss.

He tried to make it
as beautiful as He could inside, complex,

and with a simple surface
like a muscle;

something that mimicked
the complexity of life and the simplicity

of any meaning; something
that made it easier to be born and die;

as important and balanced
as anything could really be.

He created the family
and handed it out randomly to His creatures.

The birds and the mammals,
for example, all said thank you. They knew

it surpassed intelligence
in refinement,

in terms of what it could do.
Fathers and mothers held each other tightly,

their children gathered around them lovingly,
all sublimely competent and content.

At the edge of the field
stood two trees

too close together:
an oak and a pine.

Their masts interpenetrated;
every fiber vied with a force

that couldn't be recognized.
This grand game of go,

the animals sighed,
is like our own lives.

Growth and antigrowth.
Sight overwhelmed by blindness,

and roots by thirst.
The shepherd replied,

All consciousness fights
against itself. These trees

have no enemies, only
more or less leaves.

An unidentifiable animal
in an unidentifiable sequence of time,

with no apparent effort of her own,
began reciting. My thoughts fall

like paint splashed across a wall;
what I know is form, and wisdom

is the image, seen but unculled.
Why do you rate? The animals were irate.

What there is comes from you, she replied.
Your own explosiveness can't be denied.

As each individual flares out, the wise
simply uncover their eyes and see.

There is no world of intellectual harmony.
Just individuals exploding, and others seeing.

Children die first
throughout the universe.

The aged live on forever.
Animals never

get their terms straight.
Man relates

to *what* he is eating.
He thinks he gets older

by living longer!
When he says good-bye

to his mother,
said the shepherd,

she is bending over like the sky
and crushing freedom.

Around the field
where the animals lay,

around the brook,
the ocean, hill and sky,

around the tree,
around the mound,

forces were at work grinding.
They are attacking

our medium! The animals were scared.
The world is at war!

Help comes
after the attack, not before.

The shepherd said,
An army always has one thing

in common, making it move.
This army is in search of love;

it will murder for love,
destroying homelife, the man and wife.

And children watch it approach,
nits armed with motes.

Do we ever stop learning?
one animal posed. I am about to die,

my life cycle has come down to the surface,
and yet I am still gaining from it.

New ways arise of making life more firm
and pleasant; nothing any longer comes

as a surprise. Confusion, betrayals,
the lies and stagnation,

are simply inflations and deflations
of limitlessness—having no effect.

Here am I, fast approaching the throne
where no one sits: a voice wrapped in force.

When animals sleep,
they are bound hand and foot;

once awake,
there is no way for them

to regain contact with their bodies.
In between these two states

lies innocence wherein
the animals float

like vapor in a tank.
This is our context,

they told the shepherd.
This is our home. Between

those asleep
and those alone.

What they had on had
a general purpose: It eventually

would sadden them all.
Faces whose subtle lines were moral.

These were compliant and obedient,
terribly shy, afraid to be lax,

inhibited in a strict order. But
their little lies added up to another life

which gaped, throbbing
like a beet-red organ in back.

These masks had the order of art
and, having made the animals spirit, cracked

slowly and piece by piece
dropped into a pit

of turds and debris.
The animals emerged

into a world of betrayal
where their actions were free.

There it stood before them all:
the Platonic rendering of an animal.

Part of the wind and soil;
so dry and tense and unbelievable,

yet filled with individual slumber.
Through it could be seen the clouds

and fields and the sun as a dead egg.
The shepherd raged, This sum

of all our common characteristics
is the basest form of mathematics:

structure searching for a structure;
a number becoming number and number.

Every sound makable
somebody had made

at one time or another:
whether moo, cackle, roar

or other voice; whether
adventitious sound from the skin

rubbing; whether cry of agony
or love sound; they were made.

The shepherd said, Watch
as the world responds to every sound.

Its heart opens like a fresh wound.
We can hear it: Give me more! Communicate!

Feed my meaningless state.
Sound moves through every medium,

but only an animal can turn
medium into miracle. The only warm sound.

The animals pleaded: Please,
tell us that story about the magic tree.

The shepherd leaned against a trunk.
He motioned them to be seated.

All complied. Once upon a time,
he said, in a land without misery,

there grew something new, a tree
with blue leaves and golden bark.

It carried wisdom like a lark
in its boughs. Anybody who approached

left knowing something that could not possibly
have been, something hard as a diamond.

There were no fruit nor snakes around,
nothing more profound or relaxed

than the delicacy of the branches.
Their detail cleared the mind.

That tree is still there.
None of us has ever left its garden.

None of us ever need learn
how to be pardoned. Nor

how to find where we never were.
The animals felt better.

Prophecy is hidden in the function
of machines, the animals complained.

Quarks and charms,
gluons and gravitons,

these are nothing but gears
spit out by gears!

Our hearts hurt,
and no vision explains how or why.

We prefer our own language
of grunts and calls,

a science of expectation
no science can describe.

The animals were yearning for
a wider vocabulary. Your words

are the same that we hear
from simple shepherds, they claimed.

We hunger for the latinate, for terms
fanciful, descriptive and arcane.

A *mot juste* for just us few.
The shepherd proclaimed, The truth

is most complex when simply stated.
It is the plain tone that gives form

to what we need to hear and learn.
Insights are naturally clear and firm.

Flowers were rife
in the field.

The animals mustered
a philosophical question.

Why do their colors
perfectly match? they asked.

Within and together,
they give

such harmonious pleasure,
while we cannot even stand

close to one another.
The shepherd had the answer:

Flowers bare no inconsistencies;
they all breathe

from the same source.
We animals are worse.

Our own organs clash; we chase
every breath into the depths.

Light was food.
It was *the* mood

that meant.
Eternal vibration

unsent.
Blind, the animals

saw it connect space.
Grace, ungraced.

Sight! We must see!
Send us a new process

with less meaning,
they pleaded.

Every move
could be described

then added to
the previous move

until with death
description was complete

biography.
But underneath,

all the animals grieved
for an unbelievable story,

unique, friendly,
and radiant with glory.

The horizon is a skin
so thin,

the shepherd commented,
that where it divides

can hardly be seen.
And yet, the animals rejoined,

it was our first order,
our only border,

a line that always changes
but can never break,

an unavoidable barrier
to the beyond.

The shepherd knew that in his body
there were small screws

and that underneath the clouds
the rain gathered its poison mounds

of clear air. Certain plants even
contained sacraments from before lava.

The universe whistled and sighed
when the sorcerers were high

and yielded its insights of revenge
and young beauty. He said,

Ritual is the fear of magic,
and magic is fear of the tragic.

Every animal reacts to another's death
magically. So do the clouds and trees.

What have we learned?
the animals muttered.

Has anything come out
of this? Somebody said,

Like a knife that goes dull
without ever having cut,

our minds fell under
the influence of that shepherd.

He taught us that we peer
constantly into a new distance where,

sad and confused, we await
our first sharp moment.

The flock rose in full rebellion.
They had had enough of the shepherd's reason.

You split hairs into hairs! they screamed.
You view our world as your wet dream.

Every event must be positioned, evaluated,
timed. Life must be triturated between

the teeth of your mind! This field is ordered,
not reasoned. Dummy, it has no borders.

You cannot stand on the outside looking in.
There is no such thing as a proposition.

The animals had chosen
a lower form of life

to guide them.
Endowed with intelligence,

the shepherd could engage
in language,

stimulate and lay barren.
He could reason!

But, they wondered,
can we stand this shame,

being entirely innocent?
Man,

who kills his children
then weeps like a baby,

was made to suffer
his own abuse, one animal said.

We must study hard
what to avoid.

The shepherd was depressed.
He confessed to himself:

There is no way
that I can be a leader.

All these things I say
come from nowhere.

I cannot regulate
my own life or face anything

with precision, calm and clarity.
I am a beggar,

reliant on the animals
for charity.

Inadequacy is the fight
against what we are,

said the shepherd.
It is the realization

of imperfection, the source
of emotional disorder.

There can be no remedy
except as a matter of degree.

The animals disagreed:
Inadequacy is a disease

of human values. *We*
can be happily complete,

they said, liberated.
Survival is the proof

that we are whole.
There is no such thing

as an inadequate
animal.

All of the animals
were constantly busy,

their entire lives
permeated with activity.

Such refined release,
the shepherd marvelled.

Such value and peace.
So much gained and lost

in the same motion.
Such tender accomplishment

and emotion in the act.
The animals continued

their resplendent tasks,
and a temple emerged

to enhance,
yet counterpoise, fact.

Only death
is instantaneous,

said the shepherd. Ease
is the ability

to relax as moments
contract and expand.

The animals replied,
Only one moment ends,

it's true.
We always

have another chance,
until we don't.

The maze lay before them
in the grass and on the waves.

This complex motion
was the meaning they craved.

We see these nerves
forging through tranquillity,

they said. Signification
is the dharma of wind.

But, the shepherd questioned them,
what is the essence of this meaning?

The animals replied, This wind
rises up out of its medium into the mind

and is identical to the original form
of quiet. It is the impress of quiet.

At the end of
the first act

white blossoms
emerged. The

light was thrown
back

on the audience.
Then came the

crisis.
The animals sensed

the bush break,
taking chances

just before the
intermission.

When the hero
reascended toward

the end, he was
tiny, purged,

and desperate
for friends.

An animal lay under a tree
on her death bed, filled with regret.

My life was too short, she said.
I was given too much. Fed.

Everything I told my body to do,
it did. Why was I so unlucky?

Only the outside got in my way.
But now, too soon, the inside is leaving me.

My entire experience unfolds before my eyes,
one small event after another, eventless.

I never got what I needed.
There was nothing to get. It was too small,

too forgettable, unnoteworthy and cruel.
And now it is almost over, immovable.

If I could only do it once again,
I would deny myself, forfend the offering.

I would let love in its tiny pools flare
by the harsh light of my created obstacle.

Ants were attacked from above.
Eagles from below.

Frogs from behind.
Zebra from the side.

They all complained
to the shepherd,

What they want to steal
is ourselves. From any direction.

To take us away and use us.
There is a purpose in their action,

an inherent advantage unknown to us,
connected with taste.

The shepherd said, The faster
death comes, the more precise.

Life was made in a storm.
There it suffers best.

The animals were waiting to participate
in something exciting and different.

We need glamor! they clamored.
Luxurious pleasure. Satisfaction and fame

at the same time. Thrill with completion.
Success and calm.

The shepherd replied: Glamor
is like a ghost with false teeth

that shine in the dark. Everyone remarks
who sees the movement of the gums

how someone now frightening and ludicrous
was alive once.

Many animals piled up lives
in accessible areas

in order to feed
more conveniently.

Some needed their sleep.
Others were afraid of night.

Some were lazy. Others
were malicious and crazy.

The shrike said, My hangings
are part of the public domain.

The bee said, Sweet and gold,
I gather potentiality.

The man said, I am gathering
emptiness in order to succeed.

Stacks caused new stacks,
and blood fed blood.

The animals shuddered before the Bomb.
This Bomb is more than death, they said.

It is birthlessness!
It is an infinite scar. It brings life down

one level of detail toward the void.
The animals all huddled around:

What can be done about the Bomb?
One day it will eat earth.

Defense must be left to the loose cells
invisible among stars.

Some of our fellow beings
are turning into poultry,

the animals complained.
It's raining cats and dogs!

Buffalo are phasing into cows.
Turds are by-products. Milk

is a commodity. Fruits
are being crushed into drinks.

The air's not fit to breathe.
The water is green. Where

are all the trees? This place
is filled with aridity!

The shepherd laughed. If they
only live longer, he said,

if they only become stronger,
we can all get away.

A combination of plain speaking
and embarrassment since

there was no other way.
The only acceptable pose: automaton,

in their age. Blind, chewing on newspapers,
moving through the day like tanks,

in flanking off Asia, how could they
read and repent at the same time?

All the animals whined:
Shoot me. Shoot me. Shoot me.

There was no other way
to escape the glacier.

A psychic of the herd could see
into the thoughts of all humans.

What they think from day to day
is like what stirs at the bottom

of a sink, she said. Ordinary,
ugly, destructive and boring muck.

Mysterious: why the rest of us
have had to suffer such rotten luck.

The ironies of existence had no need
to be so crassly employed.

The shepherd was curious.
How will you survive, he asked,

in the face of man's destructiveness?
The animals were amused: We were given

the key, instinctively.
Men are known to us by the wildness

of their intentions. Every one of them
was born with a *mission*, a compulsive insanity

that dominates and determines his humanity.
Each man struggles against himself, relentlessly.

Ignorant of their own goals, they
can be controlled. We give them what they want:

plenty of room for their toys,
their filth, their weapons and their graves.

Grievously struck
by sinew and fang and claw,

he lay on the ground,
waiting for the performance.

A newness came through
and began sewing.

Up, up, the body rose.
The pain was acting serious.

Delirious, the mind expressed
itself: I have nothing more to do;

interaction within my wound
is like the miracle of the first sun,

shining and healing,
firing soul and body into one.

I am broken. But untaken.
The shepherd commented:

Perhaps. Perhaps. And then again,
strangeness is at war under the skin.

Victory belongs as much to the loser
who can't rebuild. There is comfort there.

On the smallest level,
where elements are most fragile,

the animal had failed.
I tried to relate to her,

he claimed. I kissed her
then froze.

Everything I wanted,
I wanted too much.

A well of emotion rose,
boiling with thin scars

and containing something
seared beyond recognition.

Something once soft,
delicate and in position

to give. Something
now dead, inside,

flailing
its uncontrollable arms.

The deeper the shepherd
penetrated, the more lost he became,

the closer to nothing.
This weave of meaning

isn't covering anything,
he moaned.

It has no intrinsic function.
The texture hardly

holds together.
Within tide, wind and flame

voices rise,
praising blindness.

The shepherd had a pleasant dream.
In it he saw the animals unwind

into a world where art was *understood*!
A shining land of apprehended meanings.

If what we do can last to be incorporated
into our understanding, he thought,

at last there will be achievement
and true social advancement.

While now the blindness is so extreme
that in all of the kingdoms art is gone,

if we could simply divine, refine, soften,
we need never again be miserable and wanton.

In the back of the throat
where the mouth can't reach,

a mammal begged to be sucked
and pleased. My milk boils

to receive any pleasure offered,
it pleaded. Pulsating delight.

I want to respond so deep,
beyond any measure, sense, or spirit.

Mortal pleasure is a hard seed.
Painful pleasure, kneading infinitely.

I am crazy for love.
Give me. Give me.

The shepherd responded:
Yours is no way to caress loneliness;

the lightest, most excited touch
is simply what it is. Below the surface,

pain is maintained
and gives out short, exquisite bursts

to reinforce its kingdom, then
rises stark out of the flames of orgasm.

The shepherd was dismayed.
I can feel age inside

as a constant, he said.
A hollowness and dread.

Time does not change.
Change cannot change.

Only our isolation,
which hardens and deadens, grows.

The requirements of our love
become less and less,

turning into hope.
And death becomes a simpler thing:

too simple
and understandable.

Life is simply a series
of yes and no decisions;

those beyond conviction
are only required to provide answers,

one animal said. The great delusion
is to become involved

in the illusion of involvement. Interest
emanates from distance; deterioration

can be fascinating if impassibly studied.
When the mind dies,

the last thing to go should know
what else has gone.

The vision was compressed
against their faces. Each

was all ready to stop. Muscle solder
coming apart. Breathing in

and breathing out too complex
and the breath caught. Thought

became imponderable and lost: They watched
the world unfurl and jerk, then halt.

Where are we? Where are we?
They were now asking the worst question.

We are impossible to be! This canvas
is filled with a black fire

whose gold tip smolders
like rope in our chests.

Lined up in boxes
of all sizes,

a hot spray rose from their mouths.
Who made you this way?

the shepherd questioned. What they
took away, nobody can find.

The animals responded, We are paralyzed!
Here, inner space has no final dimensions

in terms of the outside.
We simply are. Boxes.

Our desires flow through like rivers on fire.
Unconsumable boats breathe the fumes

from the banks, immovable.
We can feel the cold air above descend

and tingle. A magician took something
useless and left us. Our world

seethes, the boiling currents wheeze
in our lungs. Only our confidence is gone.

The animals were buried
in darkness. They called,

Let there be light! Then,
the darkness was turned into night.

Bewildered, they begged
for further substitutes. Even when it's bright,

there is a hollow here, they cried,
and we can't see. Suddenly,

light showered down in fantastic
bubbles. The dark crumbled

and flaked away on a cold
wind. It was getting old.

Even this dies, they marvelled.
Something killed it. Something black.

The sky was like the bottom
of a pan on fire. The moon,

a smoking hole. Embers danced
from the level of the land, upward.

Trees gave off the flames of dreams,
and the ground crawled, frightening.

This was a storm, at the height
of terror and suffering. Nighttime

delusions crackled in the air.
The animals were informed in a nightmare.

They whimpered, too scared to groan.
Monstrous, incredible, the cinch tightened.

Out of every possibility comes terror.
We are never secure! Never!

There is absolutely nothing to reach for,
to protect. No one to nurse us. We are neglected.

The shepherd said, Pain, the vampire, is overhead.
Feed it blood, not spirit.

The bottom of the well is dark and still.
Pain rises up like a miasma, thirsty.

Swords flew
through the air until they burned space.

The trees were all sodden
and sagging badly. The lion

was trying to reason with the camel.
This is the way it was intended to be, he exclaimed.

Those orange clouds boiling over
red.

In an endless tunnel,
hiding from the necessity

of going through, the animals
were experiencing pain for the numberless time.

Why can't it present its own specific
world drawn on the basis of nuances? Of infinite structures?

It is so awesome
coming from somewhere we can't be!

The earth was shaking, windows
were splattering on the ground. The trunks

were twisting like snakes,
vomiting.

The shepherd watched the animals
stagger through the storm.

One vast swarm of life clawing
for footing. He surmised:

Only the concept of order
is permanent. The eye

looking through itself,
its own ability is the only thing

that stays. The animals screamed,
There are no standards,

no guides. Nothing
tries to become what it is!

All the animals looked
over their shoulders for the sight of God.

He started the whole thing!
But this concept passed every one of them by.

Who is this God Who
more than once robbed me of a meal? they said

in unison. He certainly hides himself a great deal
from our thoughts! Why doesn't He cut in on the line?

Especially if He is Love;
but then we couldn't function.

All the animals rose up toward God
in a bloody pile.

The red color had a certain
religious beauty.

All had gone down
and bubbled up

like boiling water.
Everything they had they lost.

Their fondness and goodness,
their beauty and softness,

all had gone down,
died, then rotted.

This storm showed the way,
the shepherd stated.

It reduced everything
to the same thing.

The most delicate child's
tear is no more.

Out of the animals
came a new set completely different.

What did they have in common
now that the first set was dead?

The second set pondered—
long enough to die.

We are getting close to the end
of our ropes,

said those that remained,
who couldn't remember names.

Somebody keeps breathing into our ears,
said the earless ones. We can't concentrate!

A new animal arose meanwhile
but nobody noticed,

and a virus began developing
to provide some control. There is no end

to this, they despaired. No end at all.
The long view is way too long.

Fear is when we need to know
something we don't know,

said the shepherd.
It is as simple as that.

Take our sun. It shines
into the bowels of space. A grain,

a small irritant. What
we perceive as pain, out there

has no bearing but a faint twinkle.
Yet somewhere, the fear,

the same blankness and distance,
surrounds all new questions.

Scrambling through the biosphere,
the animals resented its veneer.

We add up to a sense of direction,
they said, while on the inside

our madness stays unsuppressed.
We are the definition of chaos.

The shepherd admitted, The first person
is the source of disorder and delusion.

From one view, reality is always skewed.
But nothing seems chaotic at a distance.

The outside of the stars is smooth and spare.
At the far reaches, they twinkle, ordered.

The universe is perfection
since it holds together nicely,

claimed an animal in the herd.
The shepherd overheard:

Perfection indicates the existence
of imperfection. There is no strength

in wholeness, no integral differences that hold.
There is no harmony without notes.

Is pain perfection? Or disease?
When the raptor swoops, who is pleased?

And who isn't? Life
is beyond the coverage of policies.

Beyond perfection. Beyond harmony.
Nobody has, or needs, the courage to be.

If this is space,
they said,

then time
is movement.

If this is time,
they said,

then space
is rhythm.

If this is both,
they said,

then we
are torn.

If this is neither,
they said,

then we
were never born.

Constantly, they had to remake
the rules

in order that they conformed
with their schedules:

All the food
had to be eaten and a line

drawn between sleep and waking.
The weakest had to be crushed;

the strongest permitted to suck.
Communication was limited to essentials

and songs, children protected first.
Emotions enforce our social order,

they said. Fear and hatred
maintain our borders while love grows.

Within our groups,
harmony is simply what works best,

and heresy is
synonymous with death.

Nobody could understand
the natural progression.

On one side of the universe
a cell would divide.

On the other side, a cell
would get out of the way.

Did one come from where
the other went? The fundamental

relationships never changed.
The shepherd said,

Some animals think they change
but that the sum never changes.

There is no sum. The sun
defines its own brightness

where there are no days. In the same
way, one can never know a total.

The process is highly local:
We come from where we go.

The animals took what they wanted,
ripped pelages, stole the milk, decamped

with the vegetables. We've gained!
They yelled and screamed and danced.

We are ahead by this much! Greed
is not an impulse but a method.

Those that suffer the worst are stunted:
slow to reflex, destined to be denied.

One must have the will to grab, to arrive.
The shepherd commented, Your greed

arises from the need to be empty. These objects
will drop, one by one, as you starve.

Every animal now knew
that being an animal

had never been natural.
There is something here,

they deduced,
that refuses to appear.

It caused this whole thing
willfully, in order to prove

an obscure point:
constructing scant ironies

for an audience
of furies.

The animals made to possess
were jealous.

There are actually some
with no home, they complained.

Certain animalcules and men.
Free of lifeless ends.

So, better the integrity
of the body, independent.

The shepherd responded, Anybody
can buy poverty for a price:

everything one has
and everything one is. But

poverty must be
precisely what one wants.

An apricot tree was growing
nearby. The shepherd plucked

a fruit. This large seed
lacks sweetness inside, he said.

Otherwise, the fruit is consistent
from the skin in. Fulfilling

and transient. It is the seed,
dark, mysterious and unexpellable,

which breeds, unwanted. So we
are like these fruits, hanging

from one thread, unknown. Carrying
something unknowable, which must go

after us. When we die, it grows
and lets down new threads.

Are we alive or is this a dream?
The animals were nervous and unseemly.

Sometimes our bodies float away,
they said. We wake up at night half here,

half there. Torn between corpse and spirit,
we cannot imagine ourselves. Half-witted,

we see only one side of each issue,
like dreamers. The shepherd replied,

Each dream is a lie
which cannot exist as a dream.

What is a dream? It is a dreamer dreaming.
Where is the dreamer? And what is he *doing?*

Without a dreamer, the dream becomes *real.*
Then waking is finding, claimed the animals.

It never
changes

yet is never
the same.

It identifies
itself by name.

Within,
it once bled its

still, spotless
blood.

Now emptied,
the shepherd said,

it is its
own food.

Their time had been wasted,
turned sour just before

it came to pass
and then hurried past.

Now days fly
hysterically by

and wait patiently
on the other side

to degenerate,
the animals complained.

We are impotent
in the most complete sense.

The animals said, Your immortality
is assured, since you're the shepherd!

We are simply held by ligaments and bones,
our shells, chitinous structures and skins,

in a network of convergent lines,
the geometry of nonexistence.

But you will continue after death to have
significance. While we degenerate. Now,

you are the paste in the scrapbook of our lives,
they insinuated with nasty animal humor.

You are making yourself better and better,
so that soon we shall move onto the page

as our photos wither and unply. This page
of your biography, carved in the sky.

The animals wandered away,
sick to their stomachs.

Wait, the shepherd yelled.
I have more to say!

They grimaced. All you do
is tell us your idea of truth,

which from you means
the ultimate pomposity.

Truth is not what
can be said. It is

our method, and yours,
and the earth's. It is

the way it tells itself
so it can't be told.

All this learning
is getting boring,

the animals claimed.
Word after word,

sentence after sentence,
with no build-up,

no drama, no climax,
no connections.

Simply insights
standing by themselves.

The shepherd said,
Dramatic action

is illusion. We live
and learn by impulse:

flash and fantasy
expressed sporadically.

The animals claimed: You stutter
and start. Your language is like farts

made out of leather, then stretched
and sometimes torn across a grate.

Underneath which meaning sinks
into a network of stinking pools.

You must think we're a bunch of fools
to buy your sense of linguistic beauty.

It is too thick, complex and nauseating.
The shepherd replied: These words

are like birds without wings in a land
without sky. Intrinsically able to fly.

The shepherd said,
I have invented a new style

that is made out of metal.
Tough and durable,

it denies prettiness
and superficial behavior.

It is aesthetic
gravure on paper:

a child's sword,
charmed by words.

We are fascinated
by our wastes,

the animals admitted,
and use them for signs.

They tell us what we were
on the inside.

These are our cairns,
sexual snares and boundaries,

the production
of our foundries.

The problem with you, Shepherd,
they said on the side,

is that you hide
your end-products.

No one can find you
or define you.

The animals were feeling low.
They gathered in a group and shuffled,

embarrassed and pensive. They mumbled,
Shepherd, your words have been invaluable,

but we need to ask one more question.
After much reflection, we uncovered

a peculiar form of self-deception:
You have nothing to believe in!

We have watched your eyes turn up, while underneath
you seem to be floating on an empty sea,

an ocean with no animal in it, made
of air and fire. Your lyre has been lost;

it is frankly as if this veil of meaning
kept you from sinking. Your words have been .

an ironic defense of your own buoyancy.
Your art, the only means of functioning!

The shepherd began to cry. He sobbed and sighed.
The search is all I have. What I know

is useless. What I do is fruitless.
It is only in my dedication to the poem

that I can believe in a home,
where artist and art are one and life is good.

Through the world they travelled,
as they travelled through life.

This pure feeling is what makes
the sky thrive, they insisted.

Our experiences form up inside
like these clouds. Heavy and bright.

Supportable and entirely beautiful.
It is our wandering that makes them fine.

Extending through time like a golden road,
our lives are filled

with challenges and animals.
The shepherd replied, Your road

has tremendous integrity and strength.
Spirits clap along its entire length.

Between now and the end
extends the Way, said the animals.

A path that slowly decays
until it is impossible to proceed

except on our knees
or that stops abruptly

or that turns round and round
or that extends down

into itself. A road
only insofar as it moves

us along. The shepherd responded,
No. It is not a road, it's a song:

one's own voice
singing *separately*

like sunlight
moving through green leaves.

The cycles of birth and death
vibrated like transverse waves

through the various animals.
Summoning them to behave and learn.

Out of this illusion and pain
emerges Atman, absolutely serene,

the Indian contingent averred.
The Christians called it Holy Spirit.

The Jews refused to name it.
Mohammedan, Sikh, Buddhist, Shaman,

all knew the meaning of quiet.
This life is supremely calm,

the shepherd said. Let us all
bow our heads and wait, silently, to fall.

Sun and wind
followed the rain.

The mist flew off the trees
and gusted up violently

into the light.
So our relationships, so light,

fly into the brightness
when we love, the shepherd said.

The animals were annoyed:
What you have described

is hardly friendship.
Here is a rainbow!

Let us see how it hangs
in the dry air.

In the darkness, that soft breath
which never leaves us is us, they said.

It is the desire to be emptied
into ourselves, to become softer.

We want our fear to turn warm,
our guilt to disappear, our knowledge to clear.

We want to leave our threats in the light.
Yes! the shepherd brightened. The best

we can hope for is to become darker.
Darker and warmer; softer; less.

He fell
through the earth,

boiled the truth
in his many eyes.

Every suggestion
was counterpoised,

guilty of reflection
upon itself, pride.

The shepherd said,
This devil is like a bee

who can't stand honey.
Helpless and lonely.

The shepherd addressed
the animals,

Immensely complex
within the universe

arises the one
to duplicate the One:

A trillion galaxies
breathing

in each atom.
In each soul

the void throbs.
In each thought

God is born
and cries out!

The animals responded:
The universe is *us*!

We are within ourselves.
Nothing else.

The beauty of an equation
is in the step it takes away

while keeping things balanced.
At the very end, the shepherd maintained,

we wind up where we began:
setting up the scales again.

The process itself
needn't be put to the test.

Logic is lovely
when it is free to molest.

An animal choked:
It felt the rope

of evolved destruction.
The universe

has pinpointed my death,
it gasped. Another predator

has been built
for my benefit;

and I shall again become
a form of income,

moving up
from where I started

under the first
gum.

Change
is what time *does*,

the animals winced.
It is simply

the inability of anything's
remaining what it is.

We live by slowness;
survival is pace.

Racing time results
only in ties.

All their energy was gone.
A weight hung

around their knees.
The love they felt had died

so handily.
They wanted so deep

just to be held and kissed
completely. They wanted

to find peace
in what had always been ordinary.

The world looked askance.
I shall give you something,

Animal, it said. Something
that both gives and takes.

I shall give you my warmth.
Enough warmth so your body quakes.

Imperceptibly, the moon
pulled away the earth's

energy. Like the cry
of a new baby,

claiming no responsibility
for what it was,

pain and pleasure headed
toward the stars.

The shepherd said,
Each moment we become

a little less and separate.
With infinite slowness

the earth relaxes,
making sharper cries.

Packs, crèches, nests,
undifferentiable masses,

colonies, schools, hives,
clusters and families:

Certain of the animals
would group.

We evolved past the limits
of individuality, they claimed,

to the point where an individual
had to be built.

Our lives require
participation

or we die,
lonely and overspecialized.

They could act naturally,
and normally would get their way,

but their involvement was so light
that their methods took them over.

They became what they taught of themselves,
selfish and strong.

The truer animals complained:
We are caught in a net. Life demands,

and we can't back out, can't back away.
Everything we attempt tugs.

Circumstance after circumstance,
it twists and thickens.

Trapped, forced to do,
to continue, to become,

we feel so worthless yet so involved—
embittered and beyond help.

The shepherd reminded them,
Involvement is the only way to keep you

active within dullness. It is the only way
to provide you with an address.

What is happiness?
the animals asked.

We haven't the least
idea. Despite your

fancy notions,
we haven't received

a clue. Is it
something new

and undiscussed?
The shepherd responded,

Happiness is
contentment.

Never again
having to guess.

Every proper decision
I ever made, an animal admitted,

was a bad guess. Why,
Shepherd, is the judgmental

process such a random mess?
The shepherd replied,

We operate in a throbbing arena
where audience and victim

refuse to play our game.
They respond only to brain impulses

whose feats are circuits.
A puppet that decides and redecides,

each martyr pleads mercy before
the gallery that never moves.

The bind was strengthened
by the necessity of identity

with what was bound.
It was not enough

to be threatened by opposites,
to have a choice

which could not quite be made
in the sense that B

could never be taken away from A
completely. What they were

and what they did
were inseparably frayed.

The shepherd said, Beyond choice
there is recognition of the unchoosable.

Inhibition must be placed outside
of possibility to be freed.

The animals naturally formed
into two groups: This

is war! By fusion.
Those ovaries demand

my emission, said group one.
Group two

had the blues
awaiting parturition.

What a hell of a system!
We need to be reconditioned!

A solid way must be found
to be free: Pleasure

never caused such agony.
Two should never make three.

Each animal worked hard
to develop a space. A space

where things could be laid,
like the ability to make love.

Naturalness they knew
as relaxation combined with truth.

One hand could clap successfully.
Inspiration, foul goat,

was the ultimate in release:
pleasing with nobody pleasing

and nobody pleased. Growth
was inspiration; and so was death.

The universal models hung over their heads,
but the animals were mostly unreceptive.

They said, It is impossible
to *become* inspired. The shepherd said,

What you *are* is inspiration,
gently released from what you were.

It was a real solstice:
the time of year when earth

renounces ordinariness.
It was raining kisses; bliss

poured into their orifices.
Down they went, heavenly fluids

coursing in muscles; their eyes bent,
stiffly receptive, perfect ornaments

for the grand vision to swoop down.
When it came, they brayed.

Birds dropped. The soil boiled.
Trees scratched the ground.

The animals imploded, becoming resolute,
hard. We are *now*! they said.

We can divine, persevere, raise the dead.
For once, a moist halo rules the world.

Then the sun passed over the line:
All voices emptied; trees straightened.

The shepherd said:
Clarity, spare force

embedding the understanding,
and necessity, most similar

to honesty in feeling and appeal,
these would make a fine animal,

at its very best
rejecting instinct as unsound.

Certain of the animals were dying
to survive. We must live at all costs,

destroying what is naturally lost,
augmenting in our own eyes

our difficulties until they rise up
nagging to tear us down.

We should try to relax while racked
on our own wheels. The goal

is to make life more complex,
more unknowable. It is through *self-doubt*

that we can blind ourselves
and march colossal to our graves.

One animal stood over the body
of another. Victory. In this case,

the fur was limp below the conquering
feathers. I have won for all time,

it howled. This life is now digestive slime.
God in heaven, show me how to change, if You can.

I need to win. There isn't a choice
that relegates morality to the sound of Your voice.

Maybe You made me what I am.
The shepherd watched it pick the spoils.

He turned to the other animals.
Valor leads to this, he said.

Define yourselves, before the world deadens.
Battle is the symbol for what we are.

But what we are is not at war. There
is a simple flower growing next to that body.

At the height of the day,
the shepherd was awakened

by a new animal
he thought he'd never seen.

Where have you been?
the shepherd queried.

In a constant state of confusion,
came the response.

But I did know you once.
And then I lost you, as you did me.

My life submerged
under a new hand and word.

I wandered alone
through a vast expanse

where, wingless and inefficient,
not one thing was ever gained.

And now I'm back after many years,
tears softer.

Maturity is independence,
the shepherd intimated.

Not being degraded by
the presence of others.

Attachments are a sickness
for which there is no cure.

We must be totally free
of all that we love and fear,

so that love and fear are simply
embodiments of what we are.

The animals responded: Only
humans have relationships.

Animals understand the power
of self-interest.

We find our enemies and friends
deep within our own sentiments.

The animals all began
in different keys.

Their harmony drove the wind
into a spasm of hatred

mixed with regret.
Where are the violins?

it commented.
The harp, necessary,

has been replaced by hearts
deadened, then mashed.

The second movement
will never come, superseded

by a chorus that won't end.
Their song insults heaven!

The shepherd listened.
This song, he said,

has accomplished its mission.
It is more like wind than wind.

As they grew,
they grew away.

They left
in order to grow others

their own way.
They betrayed

their parents.
After they were gone,

the parents saw
their children turn.

They aged
without being raised

by the lonely
dead ones.

This eclipse proves one thing,
the shepherd said.

There is something
behind everything.

See here where the face
of the moon is blocked out by light.

Without the sun
it would be invisible, massive,

hurling through space.
Necessary and lost.

But tonight its brightness is reduced
by brightness and black earth.

Every muscle vibrated slightly.
Tongue yearned to touch the tongue.

Eyes flamed with their thin heat,
and the entire body was receptive and incomplete.

I want to *be* through somebody else,
some said. To enter reality together.

I know I'm here, but with another
we could make this "here" so much larger.

Simply the pleasure of love is so refined,
so delicate yet so substantial. It is the answer.

But, said the shepherd, remember that
the slightest flaw causes the greatest damage.

No love is perfect; no love is complete.
The whole is always victim of the part.

Love. Love. Love. Love constantly. It is
the sweetness of sweetness, tasted in faltering light.

The animals were annoyed.
On the one hand, you say love

comes from dreams; then you tell us
there are no dreams. You say

we are basically quiet,
then heavy, then slight, then light.

You are filled with petty inconsistencies.
Every word you breathe comes from another place.

The shepherd wasn't disgraced.
Can you isolate inconsistency?

he demanded. Every meaning
is inconsistent with every other meaning.

Every symbol rests in its own bowl
and shines. Every laugh is without cause of humor.

Every grief sinks in the storm.
Emotion and knowledge are discrete.

Except at the end. There,
there is nothing left to rectify.

Meanwhile, no truth makes complete
sense. I have done my best to be clear.

Their anger was a force
of separation.

It divided them
into smaller and smaller

groups until finally
they themselves were parted.

The shepherd said: Anger
is the denial of affection

through judgment. The source
of venom and lightning, friction

and indignant suffering. There
is anger in anything that burns

such as
false love and stars.

One animal held high his symbol
of revolution and overindulgence.

This essential change must be made,
he said. A new order and a new creed.

In writing we want a new *style*.
In painting a new visual object.

In politics a new way of relating.
In thought a new way of ruminating.

All the animals were bored. Not floored.
They snored. The shepherd said,

Revolution is the new blossom or
step of a baby. It is fragile beauty.

Newness is not in new *ways*.
It is newness *itself*, and self-discovery.

What produces error?
the animals queried.

Whatever we do
has a certain ring

of falsity to it,
becoming unfavorable or

downright bad.
The shepherd responded:

Our errors are
the pinions of desire,

stopping action
at a point in the mind.

Mistakes are our costs,
what we think we've lost:

our virtue, gains and vanity.
But truth is what is *known*,

not done. Spotless, endless
action without outcome.

The animals for once held sway:
It is the Outside, calm and integrated,

where we should choose to integrate.
It is the feeling of food in the mouth

without feeling the food feel that counts.
The tangible expression of the Real

is never to feel feeling feel. Feeling
can have but one source, in one heart.

Pure, uncomprehending and dark.
Then harmony, like sunshine,

comes naturally, without empathy.
The shepherd's reaction was fierce:

The world was made with feeling.
It moves through what we are.

And through all others. The Bond.
Lifting the sun out of the ground.

The animals had tried
to describe a paradise

that made sense; but innocence
always led to boredom, beauty

to overindulgence, and goodness
to a maundering indifference.

Eden must rest in a glance,
they finally concluded, denuded.

It is *suffering*
that produces paradise!

Certainty in a moment of pain
and infinite contrast.

From generation to generation,
the same guilt was handed down

as parents denied the ways
they educated children into pain.

The animals complained:
Our parents could never hunt

in the accepted ways. Their grunts
became our groans. Our dreams

were haunted by their memories,
our salvation detonated by their terms.

They shaped us, kept us children
and betrayed us. The shepherd said,

Their worst enemy was time,
which children carry in their smiles.

Envy and sadness pave the way toward growth.
We need to be free of our parents' love.

Something is always moving
inside of us, the animals pondered.

Something going nowhere, slowly
strangling itself. Something alive:

The way it coordinates
simply in order to form, the way

it digests and changes, the way
it arranges and rearranges itself,

it never stops.
And even if it does, who would know?

The shepherd said, The universe whirls,
and all life is part of the rhythm.

Metabolism pushes the stars away from each other.
Metabolism is the pulse of creation.

What we feel unbuilding within
is the consummation of universal light.

Inner movement will never go away.
The outside will always be inside a new move.

Good and bad, said one animal.
Plus and minus, said another.

True and false, said a third.
Dad and Mom, said a fourth.

God and the Devil, said a fifth.
Me and you, said a sixth.

Sick and well, said a seventh.
Life and death, said an eighth.

Sight and blindness, said a ninth.
Right and wrong, said a tenth.

Here and there, said an eleventh.
Ignorance and knowledge, said a twelfth.

Happiness and sadness, said a thirteenth.
This and that, said a fourteenth.

The shepherd said, Brain and heart
fight this war. The universe

can be *controlled* by any animal
who knows all opposites are interchangeable.

Over his shoulder the animal saw
his past open its fetid maw.

This misery goes so deep, he moaned,
it is like a bottomless wound

or a frenzy to destroy myself. A thirst
for the worst ugliness and cruelty.

There is not one enjoyable memory.
The shepherd replied, Misery

is an illusion. There is no sadness;
and no past. Each moment is a dream

about your dreams. There is no one to be
miserable. Time is totally empty.

The shepherd felt the heat
rise and mushroom.

His brain heated, too.
His hands worked, neglected.

His feet, disconnected
from the rest of his body,

carried the hot meat
while it misbehaved.

I will end soon, he said.
But I will leave behind my moods:

residual warmth
in the bodiless wastes.

Carious, defeated,
the shepherd buried himself with dung,

as ritual. The animals were temperamental:
Come out, come out, they wheedled and cried.

Ineffectually. Over his grave fungi bloomed.
There was a faint smell of rotten eggs

over the tomb. His epitaph read: *You* are dead.
The animals, disheartened and featureless,

headed back to the field.
Once there, they put up pictures and signs.

He died for our sins or because
we didn't understand, some said.

He will come back to us with his wounds healed.
Others searched inside themselves

for the Spirit. Another washed its bowl.
He was truly noble, said his successor.

He tried to hurt us.
He always saw to it that the herd was properly slaughtered.

The animals convened and nominated
a new chief. This shepherd, they said,

hasn't been dead enough.
It was mean of him to mean.

We need something lustreless,
heavy and stable to lean on.

A dogma built on ancient thought,
thought so old

that it doesn't have to be bought,
just sold. We need logic,

to the nth degree, carefully built
on acceptable fallacies,

on any type of safe group thinking,
some glamorous form of self-identity

that bellows our sex, race, creed.
Good old-fashioned animality of thought

is what we need. Now over there
stands a likely candidate:

vile enough, polished enough.
Are you an animal that we can trust?

He needed a job.
Was willing to work without wage.

He wanted to boss around.
This was enough pay.

And so he donned a cloak
with neither fur nor feather.

He found himself a herd
that was under the weather.

Here I am! he exclaimed.
Here to keep you in line.

The animals hooted, howled and hissed:
Animal hypocrite!

From his neck hung something
that too much resembled limbs

of birds or deformed ears.
His dreams were fairly regular,

revolving around eating
inedible parts. And his liver

beat wildly like the heart
of someone in heat.

Whatever he said, beyond dispute,
could only be taken constructively.

He had charisma. They couldn't deny
his right to an image beyond the ordinary.

Such a beautiful leader, they all sneered,
from whom we hide his own worst fear.

Underneath the ground,
the confusion

seemed unbearable.
The shepherd waited.

Overhead he heard
hooves and mouths.

There is no space
below, he said.

Only interaction.
Nothing down here

is dead! I
had better arise.

My only option is
to forget.

When their backs were turned,
he returned.

They were all listening
to the new man.

We shall continue to follow
whomever we can, they commented,

and this new shepherd might serve
our purpose. Truth has its substitutes.

The shepherd whispered,
These children have learned

less than I have underground,
where nothing becomes nothing.

The new shepherd ran. The shepherd
had returned. Full of knowledge,

covered with dirt. He began
the recital of all that he'd learned.

Alone in the ground, I had time
to consider what I had missed.

Had life been a closed fist
or tireless space? Endless blackness

moved in like a vise, then out again
through intergalactic distances!

In the ancient halls of my grave,
faint nebulae hung within inches.

First I had stiffened
into a shrieking hulk,

my hands had clawed up, my muscles
knotted like small lumps at the bottom

of a steaming cup, while in my bowels
a separate demon hunched, clutching

a tape. Once out, he waved back cheerfully
at the cloudy grimace and bolted into the dirt.

But a third force remained. Hovering below
the surface. The digger, the dug, the dirt,

and the purpose: It was the real death. Not
Death, nor the dead; a breath, but halted.

The shepherd told of the light
that poured onto his gravesite,

a solenoid from above filled
with truth and love. I peeked

out of the turf to see if it
were sunny, he recited. It was night.

The moon was covered with a patch.
The stars were glowering swatches,

and each called to me,
beaming a share of its destiny.

I still had been given a choice!
My own heaven of infinite recourse!

This birth seemed not much different
than any other birth.

Except for the song of the stars,
welcoming a shepherd.

The limits of sensation receded into a vast emptiness
and left me weightless, the shepherd explained.

Climbing, climbing up to where the stars breathe
their fragrant mists, I found new lightness

and saw the grasses reaching up from my mound.
Their wands were like hands. The dark was like

another dark once: Above I heard breath!
Where was I going? Into what new life?

And then I finally sensed the beauty of Her voice.
Its message, its source that filled the first void.

I saw that my life was that mound on the ground.
Where did it come from, how far down?

When the unformed forms, it must name itself and be.
It cannot see itself, just see. Her voice sang.

Her voice cannot be heard,
the shepherd stuttered.

It is that still energy that still
moves everything. The one movement

that keeps the present moving. Skill.
Knowledge. Change that is form.

It is the song we call desire:
chaste, limitless. The voice that hears!

Death leaves us in the universe.
We are what we are. Her voice is ours!

Now, there was nothing he could do,
nothing say, that explained why he moved

the way he did and why
something deep inside him sighed.

I want this so badly, he said, I died
for love of it.

Even if every animal stood in my way,
my craving would increase, impel me

toward the goal, stronger.
What is it? the animals implored.

What could turn you against us
so suddenly? Sex? A drug? Money?

The shepherd looked down. Something
within my next breath, he confessed,

makes me impervious, fills me with charity,
and makes my future seem an easy joy.

The excitement carried naturally
within the body

split into smaller and smaller
channels, like bronchi,

eventually becoming indistinguishable
and nonextinguishable.

It flattened against the sky,
turned it blue, then entered it

and became the sky itself.
When it reenters the body

as air, the shepherd warned,
it will still be pure.

It is like
wind over a lake:

the breath of peace
filled with the warmth

of day. Such waves
are small nerves

whose pleasures
are simply water,

the shepherd said.
Acted upon

but terribly calm
with one another.

It is when we die,
the shepherd proclaimed,

that we actually go away.
But the illusion isn't destroyed.

It's replaced. With what??
The animals had never been as curious.

With another minute! the shepherd responded.
Selfless, lucid, free and infinite.

There is no end to what there is,
or was or will be. One thing

occupies everything. And every time.
When we die, it remains nothing.

Vision arrives
at its own conclusion,

said the shepherd.
It is the vision itself.

This great mystery
becomes greater, more mysterious,

as our vision clears
until vision disappears

in its own clarity.
The animals said,

Sometimes we scan the heavens
looking for answers.

The more stars we see,
the more beauty.

These huge balls of energy
burning unreachably

are patient and mute
neighbors.

There is always
one, the shepherd

said, sensing.
Light

is medium.
Death

does not   •
exist. Space

is grace.
Song

cannot
go wrong.

The shepherd was counting minutes
as they unfolded within the shadows.

The meadow would occasionally part
and release insights. Timeless flashes

among the waving branches and grasses.
These experiences, he mused, are essence,

totally unconnected to events. Expressed
without meaning or location. The intense

flow of a river at a point. A diamond
on the water. Hard liquid. Light

that blinds. Within the structure of our lives,
it is supreme power, unbearably bright.

The shepherd took the uninitiated
into his grasp, aside. He said,

Inside light I found
fertile ground,

and in that ground
I found a seed;

inside the seed
darkness had been born

and wanted to emerge, unwanted;
within that darkness I found

perfection,
alive and ungrown.

They were getting closer
and closer.

Hewing, nicking, picking so
eventually it emerged

on its own. Unbelievable!!
they screamed. We tried to entitle

our rights to it,
while the meaning itself formed

out of what it was,
this imprecise method!

The shepherd said,
What it is is what

it means.
Separated from the means

of making it
by meaning itself.

It wasn't
absence. It wasn't

devotion. It wasn't
even peace

or the attainment
of anything.

It was not perceivable;
it was never

felt.
The animals waited

patiently
for the descent.

It will never come
down, said the shepherd,

to where it is.
It is

too calm
to move.

The shepherd said,
There is no connection

between its design
and apprehension.

The braille of values
blinds the fingers

so that the eye
can see the hand:

flesh become symbol,
sight and definition.

Death separates the living
from the living,

the shepherd said,
and not the living

from the dead.
It is simply the space

between minds,
a current transition.

When we die,
we enter that place

between lives
and realize accomplishment.

Within each kiss and breath,
we sense a dead,

magical distance
of peace and brilliance.

It was when the last recourse
had been abandoned and the heart

had been drained, when everything
they loved had been destroyed in some way,

when there was no proper action,
no escape and no feeling but misery.

Then, very lightly, it came.
Nothing is left to hinder us!!

the animals proclaimed, never so amazed.
Each event is unattached, indecipherable,

final, completely new, yet delible.
And when we all go down,

the music will play
free of animals and their songs.

Back and forth it goes
in perpetual motion,

a heart
with no muscular limitation,

a force that holds
the grasses in the ground,

a median
to which stars orient.

It is here!
they cheered. Its presence

is within the realm
of our senses.

Breadth and life are one.
Track and pendulum.

Every second their blindness
decreased until sight became

the only possibility.
These moments are finally open!

the animals exclaimed. We
can see beyond our vision

to where the elements of vision
themselves dance. Transparent.

There, what we are is not even
possible to be. It is too heavy.

There, it is the openness of everything,
uncontainable, ecstatically free,

that is possible. It is a stark world
of unfurled phenomena, bright and right.

There was nothing there.
Perception justified by itself.

Detail taking over the whole.
Depth risen to the surface, alone.

Over and over we repeated
the name of God, the animals said.

In each movement we uncovered
new logic and became wiser.

With every bite and breath
the world cleared, gained

in the sovereign presence
of the senses. Something.

What was it? asked the shepherd. The element
of sight? The source of light? What was perceived?

It was the clarity itself we saw,
the animals sang. Absolutely free and tame.

The animals all yearned now
for home:

to be isolated and reduced
to where they had been.

For a time we functioned
in this interstice, they said.

Learning and enjoying.
Sharing our deadness

and our lives that fuel deadness.
And the spark, entire, separate

and clear. The spark guarded
from the rest of the universe.

We made our small candles
burn bright in the black endlessness:

a galaxy
where the stars whispered.

Whatever we have done
has been for us alone,

and what we have learned
should be forgotten.

No one who can read
can change integrity,

and no one who can see
can lose what can be seen.

Farewell, fair flock
of friends and enemies.

Knowledge is the seed
that blows the wind.

They all stood in awe
before the dawn.

For a moment they
didn't have a shepherd

nor need one. We
are as free, they said

to themselves,
as this sun throwing

clarity
on the world,

rising out of the darkness
that never was.

Entwined in fiber,
stem and root;

in the first heat
of day entwined;

entwined in pulse,
stone, mote and flake;

in caverns, on peaks,
across valleys,

this face shone
with such delight,

all the animals danced
on behalf of their own insight.

The shepherd sat in the field alone.
All the animals had gone home,

leaving him to admire
the interweaving of root, branch and flower

into structure.
Their story is ended, he thought,

and they have gone on
into their own newness.

Every moment is a new animal,
more or less.

But inside this dome
of relatedness, a meaning continues

beyond all commentary expressed
by animals in their songs.

There is a longing
the fulfillment of which is truth.

The shepherd felt at ease
in a way that he had never felt

previously. What has been said
has left me, he said.

Those dead words
are out and gone, a burden

now to be carried
by the animals.

My world is emptied, free
to be nonverbal, to breathe

without sound, while the sun
attacks the shade, then dies.

Out of one eye
flow many minds, but many eyes
see through the same thing:

a stable unity,
bark
on a tree.

On the one end, rock;
on the other, sky. In between,
a fake struggle

to connect
sight with the eye.
To remain in touch as if touch and touching
were different

or seeing and sight.

Within the bleeding vale
blood forms. It is lambent and warmer.

It tells: Animal, Animal, it screams.
Feed me

what my body has to believe.

This book was set in Monotype Bembo
by The Meriden-Stinehour Press
and printed on recycled, acid-free paper
in an edition of twenty-five thousand.
It was designed by Robert Jensen
and the author.

The interior illustrations are by
Nicholas Africano.